Marketing Management: A Resource-Based Approach

for the Hospitality and Tourism Industries

Richard Teare Stephen Calver Jorge Costa

Cassell
Villiers House
41/47 Strand
London WC2N 5JE.

387 Park Avenue South
New York
NY 10016-8810.

First published 1994.

British Library Cataloguing-in-Publication Data
A catalogue record for this book is available from the British Library.
ISBN 0 304 32926 6

Library of Congress Cataloging-in-Publication Data
A catalogue record for this book is available from the Library of Congress.

Typeset by Richard Teare
Printed and bound in Great Britain by Hollen Street Press, Berwick upon Tweed

Current Titles in the Hospitality and Tourism Resource-Based Series:

Series Editor: Professor Richard Teare

- Strategic Management
- Marketing Management
- Operational Techniques
- Operations Management
- Management Skills

INTRODUCTION

OVERVIEW

Marketing management is, or should be about making marketing happen. Organizations can only succeed in the long-term if customers are satisfied and the way to ensure this is to plan, analyze, control and evaluate the marketing process.

Why a resource-based approach?
The concept of a resource-based approach to the study and practice of marketing management is centred on the need for a pragmatic, problem-solving orientation. Accordingly, the book draws from a number of existing publications in order to provide an affordable, easy-to-use guide to industry applications and examples. Industry relevance is assured by the use of detailed business cases to illustrate key principles in hospitality/tourism settings.

Readership
A key consideration in the book's design and layout is flexibility of use. It is intended as a core text for courses at undergraduate level, as a resource for open/distance learning courses and short course programmes and as a convenient, easy-to-use reference guide for managers working at all organizational levels, and in both operational and specialized roles. To ensure continued relevance, the format of the book allows for regular updating and extension.

APPROACH

Introduction
Each chapter begins with an introductory overview of the topic, followed by a contents list and related reading references which can be found in the resource publications. Access to all of the listed publications is strongly recommended.

Review
The chapter review provides a summary of key issues, influences and changes relating to the topic area. Where appropriate, industry examples are used as illustrations and in some chapters, ideas originally developed and applied in other service industry settings are used to provide a wider perspective or to explain how hospitality/tourism firms might adapt existing practices.

Conclusion and extension
A concluding statement is followed by a series of review questions which relate to the key points raised in the chapter. In most cases, the review questions test comprehension of the topic material and relevant application by requiring the reader to draw from his or her industry observations and experience. All of the extension questions and exercises are linked to marketing case problems, opportunities and other scenarios.

Teaching and learning
It is my view that the resource-based approach is flexible enough to support and encourage a range of different teaching and learning activities. These include:

(a) Reader-centred, independent study and investigation, including some self-assessment using the review and extension material. In this situation the teacher facilitates the learning activity through tutorial discussion, workshop activity and group project work involving discussion, debate and presentations, among other interactive techniques.

(b) Resource material for open/distance learning courses whereby the reader works independently at his/her own pace to an agreed learning contract. The review and extension material is suitable for self-assessment and for seminar and syndicate work whenever course meetings take place.

(c) Specific focusing on business practices and marketing management applications in hospitality/tourism organizations, perhaps as part of a wider focus on the service industry sector.

(d) As a resource for the cross-fertilization of ideas and practices, especially in relation to the way in which the extension material is used.

Summarizing, the book can be used to facilitate independent learning, direct aspects of self-assessment and to support an array of individual and group project work, ranging from the updating and analysis of business trends and company information to interactive seminar and workshop activities.

I would like to thank Stephen Calver and Jorge Costa for their valued contribution to the resource-based series and the series publisher, Judith Entwisle-Baker.

Richard Teare
Series Editor

CONTENTS

RATIONALE

It is conventionally assumed that marketing is based on logical procedures for planning strategy and tactics, budgeting for marketing expenditure on components of the marketing mix and targeting customers by collecting and analyzing marketing information. Nigel Piercy, one of the UK's foremost marketing academics sees these relationships in terms of: (a) a focus on customer satisfaction;

(b) getting marketing strategies and programmes together; (c) organizing to show we believe in marketing to customers; (d) collecting and communicating information and intelligence; (e) designing decision-making processes that work for planning and budgeting purposes and (f) implementing marketing strategies. He adds that the urgent need in most cases is to *manage* the *context* of marketing and not just the conventional content.

In giving due prominence to the challenge of making marketing happen, we have sought to balance the theory and practice of marketing management by addressing the content of the marketing process and the context in which it is applied. In broad terms, the key concepts are addressed in the review section of each chapter and applied by means of the extension questions. The five parts of the book provide a familiar framework for marketing management: marketing fundamentals like concepts, systems and organization; marketing research; marketing planning and segmentation; the marketing mix and marketing strategy. Our aim has been to explain the basics of marketing management in order to establish a foundation upon which related or more advanced studies can build. For instance, the study of consumer behaviour requires some prior knowledge of the marketing research process and the implications of research for marketing communication.

Marketing management is essentially about ensuring that customers are satisfied in the long-term. The marketing process needed to achieve this aim requires an integrative approach to managing the available resources, ensuring a customer or 'market-led' approach throughout.

RESOURCES

The following publications constitute the resource on which this book is based:

A   F. Buttle, *Hotel and Food Service Marketing: A Managerial Approach.* Cassell, London & New York, 1986. Pb. £16.99, ISBN 0-304-31533-8.

B   T. Cannon, *Basic Marketing: Principles and Practice* (3rd Edition). Cassell, London & New York, 1992. Pb. £15.99, ISBN 0-304-31673-3.

C   G. Lancaster & L. Massingham, *Essentials of Marketing* (2nd Edition). McGraw-Hill, London & New York, 1993. Pb. £14.95, ISBN 0-07-707728-8.

D   N. Piercy, *Market-Led Strategic Change.* Thorsons, London, 1991. Hb. £20.00, ISBN 0-7225-2544-3.

E   R. Teare with L. Moutinho & N. Morgan (eds.) *Managing and Marketing Services in the 1990s.* Cassell, London & New York, 1993. Pb. £12.99, ISBN 0-304-32726-3.

F   R. Teare & A. Boer (eds.) *Strategic Hospitality Management: Theory and Practice for the 1990s.* Cassell, London & New York, 1991. Pb. £15.99, ISBN 0-304-32285-7.

•   *International Journal of Contemporary Hospitality Management* (IJCHM) MCB University Press, Bradford, Yorkshire, UK. ISSN 0959-6119 (published seven times a year).

All references to the resource publications are cited in abbreviated form. For example:

•   Chapter 6 in *Basic Marketing: Principles and Practice* is cited as B: 6 pp 106-130.

•   Articles published in the *International Journal of Contemporary Hospitality Management* are cited by author, volume, number, year, and page number(s) e.g. S.J.Messenger and S.M.Lin, IJCHM, v3n3, 1991 pp 28-32.

We would like to express our thanks to Rachel and Sophie Calver, Antonio, Natalia and Monica Costa and Rachel, Anna, Matthew and Benjamin Teare for their love and support.

Richard Teare, Stephen Calver, Jorge Costa
September, 1994

Richard Teare is Professor & Associate Head, Department of Service Industries, Bournemouth University. He is Editor of the *International Journal of Contemporary Hospitality Management*, and a member of the *International Marketing Review* editorial advisory board. He has co-authored and edited eight books on aspects of managing and marketing services.

Stephen Calver is Head of the School of Hospitality Studies in the Department of Service Industries, Bournemouth University where he coordinates the teaching of hospitality marketing. He received his MBA degree with a specialism in marketing from the City University Business School, London and he is a member of the Chartered Institute of Marketing and its Hotel Sector Group.

Jorge Costa holds a degree (Licenciatura) in Business Administration from the Technical University of Lisbon. He is Head of the Marketing Department at the Instituto Superior de Ciências da Informação e da Empresa, Porto, Portugal, and is currently undertaking a higher degree by research at Bournemouth University, UK.

1

CONCEPTS, SYSTEMS AND ORIENTATION

INTRODUCTION

Marketing has a proactive consumer-led orientation which contrasts with the reactive, productivity-led approach that characterizes many contemporary businesses.

The hospitality/tourism industries have a varied approach to market-led strategies. Some sectors like branded, fast food restaurants, best exemplified by McDonald's, have a strong marketing orientation whereas hotels are often less consistent in their approach. This lack of consistency may be due to the problems of standardizing such complex service operations (see also chapter 3).

Recent intelligence (1) shows that during the recession, some hoteliers have re-considered the way in which they select and apply marketing techniques while others remain committed to cost and productivity control-dominated policies. This chapter seeks to explore these issues with particular reference to business orientation and approach.

In this chapter:
- Marketing - concept and definition
  (C: 1 pp 3-19; B: 1 pp 1-28; A: 2 pp 21-41)
- Business orientation (C: 1 p. 10-13;
  B: 1 pp 10-11; A: 2 pp 27-28)
- The marketing environment (C: 2 pp 20-45;
  B: 2 pp 29-54)
- The external environment (C: 2 pp 21-33;
  B: 3 pp 55-78)
- The internal environment
  (C: 2 pp 33-45; B: 2 pp 29-54)
- The customer
  (C: 3 pp 46-54; A: 4 pp 75-82; D: 1 pp 13-28)

REVIEW

Marketing - concept and definition
(C: 1 pp 3-19; B: 1 pp 1-28; A: 2 pp 21-41)
There are numerous definitions of marketing, many of which emphasize particular components of the marketing process. Due to the difficulty of encapsulating the different perspectives in one statement, it is important to note some of the key

points that clarify the nature, purpose and discipline of marketing:

- It seeks to focus attention on the needs and wants of the marketplace.
- It's key concern is to find ways of satisfying the genuine needs and wants of specifically defined target customer markets.
- Marketing involves analysis, planning and control.
- The principles of marketing suggest that all business decisions should be made with careful reference to and systematic consideration of the customer.
- Marketing is dynamic and operational - it requires action as well as planning.
- Marketing requires an effective form of business organization in order to lead and energize the marketing approach.
- Marketing is both an important functional area of management and an overall business philosophy which recognizes that the identification, satisfaction and retention of customers is the key to prosperity.

The consumer-led approach to business is not particularly new. Adam Smith in his book '*The Wealth of Nations*' published in 1776, expressed the view that:

"Consumption is the sole end and purpose of all production and the interests of the producer ought to be attended to, only so far as it may be necessary for promoting that of the consumer." (C: 1 p. 3.)

If the nature of marketing and its role as an essential component of successful business has been understood for so long, why do many organizations still fail to apply marketing principles? The following quote is attributed to a vice president of marketing at IBM computers:

"It's a shame that, in so many companies, whenever you get good service it's an exception. Not so at the excellent companies. Everyone gets into the act. Many of the innovative companies got their best ideas from customers. That comes from listening intently and regularly." (B: 1 p.1.)

Consider this apparently consumer-oriented approach and the fact that IBM experienced record losses in 1993 because they had underestimated the market preference for PCs. Such a phenomenon is not unusual in mature companies. Often the market place where initial success was achieved becomes a 'folk memory' and commitment to marketing principles reduced to a mantra with little organizational substance.

Market orientation requires a substantial commitment by the organization and it can be differentiated from two other broad forms of business orientation which are described below.

Business orientation
(C: 1 p. 10-13; B: 1 pp 10-11; A: 2 pp 27-28)

(a) Production orientation
This orientation is often found in markets where demand exceeds supply. Historically this situation was apparent at the time of the industrial revolution and again during the 1950s when there was exceptional worldwide demand for products mainly supplied by companies in the western hemisphere. This type of business orientation is most successful where there is limited product differentiation - in others words, where there is little difference between competing products or services. Customer requirements in these circumstances are secondary. The role of marketing in this type of company is limited to advertising and sales in the hope that the product continues to appeal to the market.

(b) Sales orientation
This type of orientation is often found in markets where supply exceeds demand, usually in companies with a heavy investment in fixed capital equipment, building and technology. Because the large fixed investment developments of new products can be costly, long term ventures can only be financed by cash flow resulting from aggressive selling of the existing product.

The hotel sector may be regarded as having a sales orientation. Supply of accommodation exceeds demand especially when the self catering sector is included in the calculation. Since hotels are immobile and structural alterations costly, they can neither be moved to locations where demand is higher nor are they readily converted to new uses such as offices, flats or retail outlets without considerable expense and risk. The focus of hotel companies is to sell what they have rather than provide what the customer wants. This practice has been further encouraged by the appreciation in property prices in the United Kingdom during the past thirty years. Until recently, many hotel companies were experiencing greater gains in capital growth than they were from their core businesses; food and accommodation.

(c) Market orientation
The modern marketing concept has evolved from the sales and production orientation, although both of these forms of business are in evidence today throughout British industry. The marketing concept, sometimes referred to as a customer-led approach or

customer orientation, began to gain momentum as a core business philosophy in the United States during the 1950s.

The marketing concept emphasizes the customer as the key to business growth and survival. A marketing oriented firm seeks to provide the goods and services that its customers want to buy. Many hotels are still intent on offering the leisure customer Edwardian style food service, reception facilities, and accommodation when sectors of the market have demonstrated a preference for less formal service delivery such as that provided in public houses and self catering facilities. The strength of the marketing approach lies in the focus on the buyer as the key component in the production process.

The marketing environment
(C: 2 pp 20-45; B: 2 pp 29-54)
An important pre-condition for a market-led organization is an effective system for scanning the marketing environment. The term 'marketing environment' is often used to denote both the external and the internal environment. For example Kotler defines the general marketing environment as:

"A company's marketing environment consists of the actors and forces that affect the company's ability to develop and maintain successful transactions with its target customers." (C: 2 p. 20.)

This definition includes all the environmental forces outside of the firm's marketing management function. This would include inter-departmental influences and overall company policy.

The external environment
(C: 2 pp 21-33, B: 3 pp 55-78)
Marketing oriented organizations must have some means by which they can routinely assess the external (or macro) environment which includes:

- Factors largely beyond the control of the firm, for instance the political, socio-cultural, economic and technological environment.
- Factors over which the firm has some influence (sometimes referred to as the macro-environment) for instance, suppliers, distributors and competitors.

The key stages of an environmental scanning system (see also chapter 13) are:

(a) Identify key environmental factors
There will be certain key issues that influence customer demand, for instance expenditure on leisure will be influenced by disposable income, attitudes to leisure and local government support.

(b) Monitor and forecast trends and changes in key environmental factors

Accessible information sources should be identified, there are likely to include: government departments, academic institutions and professional bodies. These and other sources can provide regular reports and bulletins dealing with key areas of interest.

(c) Assess the likely/potential impact of environmental trends and changes

The threats and opportunities represented by identified trends should then be assessed. This is often the most difficult part of the process. A careful analysis is required to identify the significant themes upon which decisions should be taken. Research cannot eradicate the risk of undertaking a course of action, it can only improve the likelihood of success.

(d) Plan to adjust to the external environment

Action planning requires the support and involvement of all departments and levels within the organization. This stage will be heavily influenced by the culture prevailing in the organization (see also chapter 14).

The internal environment

(C: 2 pp 33-45; B: 2 pp 29-54)

Research indicates that various factors influence the extent to which marketing policy can be successfully implemented in an organization. The key issues are:

(a) Company philosophy/business definition

Some organizations will give the impression of being market-led even when they are committed to a programme of product development which is driven by an internal agenda rather than market needs.

(b) Managerial/workforce attitudes

The flexibility and managerial style of an organization will influence the extent to which new ideas can be introduced.

(c) Organizational style

Changes in the market place may require flexibility in the organizational structure to accommodate new technology or other forms of product/service innovation.

(d) Planning and information gathering/processes for decision making

The dissemination of timely and relevant information and responsibility for developing and implementing plans within the organization.

The customer

(C: 3 pp 46-54; A: 4 pp 75-82; D: 1 pp 13-28)

In addition to scanning the marketing environment, the marketer should have some understanding of the influences that direct customer choice between alternative products and services. Influences on the customer can be broadly classified as:

- *Environmental* - the influence of culture, families and groups, social class and other societal forces.
- *Individual* - the influence of age, sex, personality and lifestyle preferences.

A determination to understand *why*, *how* and *when* customers make purchase decisions is a key determinant of effective marketing. Nigel Piercy illustrates this point by posing the question: what is marketing really all about? The answer he gives is perhaps rather obvious - marketing is about *customers*. But this reality is sometimes over-shadowed by the practice of marketing:

"Over the past twenty years marketing has become a legitimate and highly-paid professional activity in a great many organizations of all types...The business library and the executive's bookshelf show that there is a vast technical literature on the minutiae of marketing methods, concerning everything from developing computer models to support decision-makers, to psychological analyses of the motivation and behaviour of consumers, to studies of advertising media characteristics and ideal combinations of different advertising in terms of audience penetration and coverage, and so on...At the same time, in the process of becoming professionally respectable, marketing has also become a corporate way of life with its own language, technology, career path, educational preparation, training and professional identity...The point is that these trappings of marketing can also have a wholly regrettable by-product...In all too many cases we seem to have lost sight of the fact that marketing is only a means to an end. The end is customer satisfaction, not professional, sophisticated, high-technology, techniques-driven, computerized marketing."
(D: 1 p. 25.)

CONCLUSION

The hospitality/tourism industries face a number of challenges in the coming decade. These include volatile and unpredictable levels of demand, an intensification of competition and the impacts associated with the increasingly international nature of trade. Companies that retain a product-led approach in the hope that the marketplace will revert to *their* traditional approach to business may find it difficult to maintain their position in the medium to long term.

On the other hand, successful hospitality/tourism companies will have developed systems for monitoring the marketing environment and assessing customer needs. Further, the successful companies will have implemented a market-led approach in every sphere of business policy-making, planning and implementation. Piercy's assumptions about the nature of change needed to become a market-led organization (D: 1 p. 26) indicate the scale of the task:

- Organizations are forced to follow the dictates of the market (the paying customer), or go out of business when someone else does.
- Organizational effectiveness in implementing a market-led approach depends upon how successfully it is able to focus on customer needs, wants and demands.
- Market-led barriers many arise from ignorance of customer characteristics, lack of information, inflexible technology, competitive threats and, more generally, the way in which the business is run.
- A market-led approach may require an upheaval in the way an organization is structured, decisions are made, key values are communicated internally and externally and the organization's responsiveness to the outside world.
- A market-led approach amounts to a programme of deep-seated, fundamental strategic change - it cannot be accomplished by making short-term adjustments.

Reference:

1. Anon. 'Marketing, the Key to Fighting the Recession' - *Caterer and Hotelkeeper,* January 16th, 1992.

Review questions:

1. Using hospitality or tourism industry examples, explain the various types of business orientation and the factors that indicate whether an organization is market-led.

2. Outline a system, including a flow chart with management responsibilities, for scanning the marketing environment.

3. Evaluate the factors likely to influence the attitudes of 16-25 year olds in routine, re-buy purchase situations for leisure, pub or restaurant product concepts.

EXTENSION

Read: Chapter 4 of *Basic Marketing: Principles and Practice* (B: 4 pp 79-88: Structures and Dynamics in the Food Marketing Chain)

The chapter is concerned with the nature and dynamics of the food marketing system. This is a set of relationships which shape and determine the ways in which food is produced, processed and brought to market. The emphasis lies on the ways in which the ideas and thinking about marketing, the marketing concept and marketing system influence managerial behaviour, policy, technology, regulation and behaviour.

Extension questions:

1. Discuss the evidence for the contention that: 'changes in the food market are moving away from centralist and producer-oriented programmes toward more distributed and market-based programmes'.

2. Evaluate the significant factors in changing consumer attitudes and the marketing environment for which food companies should develop marketing strategy over the next four years.

3. Assess the likely impact of the changes identified in (2) above, on the organizational structure of a large food retailer. Draw an organization chart of the various management responsibilities to reflect your conclusions.

Practical exercises:

1. Prepare and deliver a ten minute presentation explaining the background to the development of marketing policy in food retailing.

2. Outline a four year marketing plan for one of the food retailers described in Figure 4.1 (C: 4 p. 83). Your submission should build on the factors that you have identified in the previous question and deal with issues such as anticipated market trends, investment in new technology and new product development.

3. From the available resources in your library, update developments in food retailing. List your references and give a precise account of each. Explain how recent developments will modify the issues discussed in the previous questions.

2

MARKETING ORGANIZATION

INTRODUCTION

The *marketing organization* is the structure, responsibilities and procedures adopted by the firm in order to manage its marketing (B: 27 p. 424). It is often assumed that structures and systems help to ensure that firms can formalize their marketing organization so that its effectiveness can be measured and continuously fine-tuned. Contrary to this, Nigel Piercy's experiences of working with a variety of organizations convinced him that this wasn't happening. So he established a programme of research into how companies organized marketing and the results they achieved. He concludes that *"...generally speaking companies do not organize to make marketing happen in any real way - even if they think and say that they do."* (D: 5 p. 134.)

This chapter sets out to examine the issues which influence the relative effectiveness of marketing organization. These include the role and scope of marketing departments, the interface between internal and external markets and the importance of integration between the two in optimizing customer satisfaction with hospitality/tourism services.

In this chapter:
- The myths and realities of corporate marketing organization (D: 5 pp 142-148)
- Marketing departments: A service sector perspective (D: 5 pp 147-151; E: 4 pp 49-73; E: 8 pp 121-136)
- The benefits of an integrated marketing organization (F: 9 pp 144-157; D: 10 pp 365-393)
- Designing a marketing organization (D: 5 pp 151-157)

REVIEW

The myths and realities of corporate marketing organization (D: 5 pp 142-148)
It is generally assumed that marketing is organized in a particular way: *The logic for how marketing issues are evaluated, for applying techniques of marketing analysis, for building marketing plans and strategies, all rests on this model of how marketing is organized (or if it isn't, how it should be)."* (D: 5 pp 142-143.)

Piercy characterizes the textbook model of the marketing organization as follows:

- *A marketing department* - its existence is assumed and that it will be formally organized to respond to market issues such as geographical areas, customer types, product groups and specialized marketing functions.

- *A chief marketing executive* (CME) - it is assumed that he or she will be a powerful figure in the company, controlling significant resources and managing the customer interface.

- *Integration of marketing functions* - it is generally suggested that all customer-related activities are co-ordinated by the marketing department and this is reinforced by the marketing programme structure as the basis for planning and managing marketing. Further, it is assumed that the CME controls all aspects of the marketing mix.

These characteristics reflect marketing organization in a comparatively small number of normally multinational companies. The reality is that most firms, especially in the hospitality/tourism industries, employ a sales force and where a marketing department exists, it is typically a small team of people who liaise with external agencies on advertising and market research matters rather than directing these activities themselves.

Marketing departments: A service sector perspective (D: 5 pp 147-151; E: 4 pp 49-73; E: 8 pp 121- 136)
Hospitality/tourism, retailing and financial services share certain common features; they assumed greater economic importance in the UK during the 1980s and arising from this, competitive pressures have steadily increased during the 1990s.

Several studies of marketing organization (D: 5 pp 147-151 and E: 4 pp 49-73 which reports on retailer marketing organizations) reveal further parallels:

- The formalization of marketing activity has, historically proved problematic because of the nature and characteristics of retailing 'services'.

- The key marketing issues are more strongly influenced by the 'organizational software' of managerial philosophy, culture, values and attitudes than by formal organizational and administrative arrangements (a 'substance' versus 'trappings' argument).

- The formal organization of marketing is indicative of much more than a means of managing customer-related activities. Structures usually reflect organizational priorities and even strategies, in that customer-related processes, procedures and systems may in themselves constitute a source of competitive advantage.

A key test of the organization of marketing is its effectiveness; an issue which is more closely aligned to a firm's evolutionary stage of development than to external competitive pressure. A study of formal marketing organizations in UK financial services firms (E: 8 pp 121- 136) provides further evidence of the existence of four distinctive types of marketing organization:

- *Integrated, full-service marketing departments* with broad-ranging responsibilities for product development and service support. This type of organization is closest to the textbook model in that they control or influence the major marketing decisions. They have a comparatively large number of staff (head-count) and a high power ranking in their companies.

- *Centralized/strategic marketing departments* with typically two or three people taking full responsibility for product policy, marketing services and corporate strategy but not for selling or physical distribution. Although this limits the scope for integrating marketing activity, the group are likely to be powerful because of their proximity to strategic issues and planning rather than line marketing decisions.

- *Selling-oriented marketing departments* with higher staffing levels but lower involvement in areas other than marketing services. They are predominantly responsible for selling and relative size means they generally have a strong influence on the running of the business.

- *Limited, staff-role marketing departments* with a low head-count and responsibilities mainly limited to marketing services. This type of department is not influential as it is too peripheral to the main business of the company.

The analysis suggests that the organizational effectiveness of marketing in hospitality/tourism firms is related to a number of factors. These include the nature and characteristics of its products and services, the size and scope of operations, the degree of specialization and the strategic allocation of responsibilities. Further, it is apparent that different types of marketing department *can* and *do* evolve

from the way in which firms perceive and address organizational priorities.

The benefits of an integrated marketing organization (F: 9 pp 144-157; D: 10 pp 365-393) A theme of Part 4 (Marketing Mix) is the need to optimize the relationships between the components of product, pricing, promotion and distribution. To sustain this effort and provide accurate information for decision-making, two-way channels of referral and communication between unit and corporate levels are essential.

Drawing from his extensive consulting experience, Nigel Piercy re-inforces the need for cross-functional co-operation:

"We have been struck forcibly and repeatedly by one major barrier to putting marketing strategies and plans into effect. That barrier is created by the people, the systems and procedures, the departments, and the managers whose commitment and participation are needed to implement marketing strategies effectively, i.e. the internal customers for our marketing plans and strategies." (D: 10 p. 366.)

If firms ignore the many points of contact at the interface between marketing, operations and other functions throughout the organizational hierarchy, a damaging 'broken chain' effect can occur. This is best illustrated by the problems encountered by American car manufacturers Chrysler, when Lee Iacocca took over as chief executive:

"The manufacturing guys would build cars without even checking with the sales guys. They just built them, stuck them in a yard, and then hoped that somebody would take them out of there. We ended up with a huge inventory and a financial nightmare." (1)

The nature of hospitality/tourism service provision requires a high degree of co-operation between production and service personnel. How then should hospitality/tourism firms apply marketing expertise to this internal network of interactive relationships?

As customer relations are continually shaped by the behaviour of service staff, they perform a 'part-time marketer' role which can be harnessed and utilized by the much smaller number of specialists responsible for the organization and co-ordination of marketing effort. The extent to which awareness of a marketing role is realized, depends in part on how successfully the marketing specialists can remove the conventional barriers that separate the marketing department from other departments and in particular, operations.

The *ideal* network can be likened to a chain whereby the internal customers from different departments and levels collectively focus on the needs of the external customer (see for example, F: 9 p. 151).

The concept of an internal customer simply reflects the many opportunities that exist for extending and integrating marketing organization. These include:

- Customer-supplier relationships, whereby groups of employees 'service' the needs of other groups as part of an integrated network.

- Disseminating and applying marketing knowledge developed initially for external marketing, to the internal market.

- Strategic initiatives to improve marketing orientation as it applies to both external and internal marketing organization. For instance, increased attention to the interface between the two, with 'front-line' service staff receiving improved sales and customer awareness training and support.

- Internal marketing which takes place when profit centres within a decentralized firm trade with one another.

Designing a marketing organization
(D: 5 pp 151-157)

Piercy identifies a number of priorities for testing the effectiveness of organizational design for marketing. These are (a) design criteria; (b) the fit with organizational strategy; (c) indicators for monitoring effectiveness; (d) implementation issues; (e) contingency planning and (f) re-organization needs.

(a) Criteria for organizational design
There are a number of key questions which can be used to test organizational design: What is the best way to achieve effective marketing implementation? How can a focus on customers and customer satisfaction be sustained? Will the organization facilitate the development of strategies and marketing programmes in order to create a distinctive, differentiated total offering to the customer?

Answers to these questions will inform initial discussions about the type of marketing department best suited to business needs and the scope and level of responsibility for *selling, product policy, marketing services* (staff selection, training, marketing planning and research) *strategy* (research and development, diversification, investment, planning) and *physical distribution*.

(b) An organizational strategy for marketing
Specific decisions relating to the organizational strategy for marketing must be made. These include: (a) specification of jobs (specializations and responsibilities); (b) span of organization (its shape in terms of levels and the resulting span of control for managers); (c) grouping of activities; (d) integrating mechanisms; (e) control systems; (f) change requirements (how will specific pressures for change be addressed?).

(c) Indicators for monitoring effectiveness
It is helpful to select the most appropriate indicators for identifying potential or actual structural problems *before* they begin to impede the effectiveness of the marketing organization. These might include indicators for detecting low motivation and morale; slow/low quality decision-making; managerial overload; conflict and lack of co-ordination; poor integration; lack of innovation; weak control and escalating administrative costs.

(d) The implementation process
The process of planning should reflect a systematic review of key business issues including: (a) analysis of the present position; (b) analysis of future needs; (c) identification of options (such as division of labour/specialization, alternatives for co-ordination and integration, model of marketing department types); (d) choices relating to specified criteria; (e) planning the implementation.

(e) Contingency planning
Contingencies for responding to future needs presents a challenging design consideration. Ideally, allowances should be made for (a) environmental contingencies (relating to forces affecting the marketplace and uncertainty); (b) technological contingencies to assess the impact of technological advancement; and, (c) corporate contingencies relating to the company's mission, strategy, culture and forces affecting its structure both from internal and external sources.

(f) Re-organization issues
The need to reorganize in response to change may create a need to allow for: (a) costs of re-organization (such as staff turnover and missed business opportunities); (b) internal political constraints (resistance to change and what may be needed to counter it); (c) an implementation plan to define the actions needed and the control and evaluation procedures to be used.

CONCLUSION

This chapter has sought to provide an overview of the issues affecting organization for marketing, with particular reference to its ability to support and sustain market-led change. This is a key determinant of marketing effectiveness as an inadequate or inappropriate type of organization will impede marketing effort. Piercy concludes:

"Either because we cannot do anything about it or because we think it is not the most urgent issue in marketing, we may face a future of driving market-led strategic change in a company with no supporting marketing organization or even more difficult, with the 'wrong' or inappropriate marketing organization. This may sound defeatist, but experience suggests that it is a practical reality." (D: 5 p. 158.)

Reference:

1.   L.Iacocca (with W.Novak). *Iacocca: An Autobiography.* Bantam Books, New York, 1984, p. 162.

Review questions:

1.   What are the advantages and disadvantages of the various types of marketing organization? How do the operational characteristics of large hospitality/tourism firms affect the type of marketing organization most suited to their marketing needs?

2.   Evaluate the importance of the 'part-time marketer' concept to hospitality/tourism firms.

3.   Explain, with appropriate examples, the concept and operation of an integrated marketing organization.

EXTENSION

Read: Diagnostic 3: 'What Type of Marketing Organization Have We Got?' in Chapter 5 of *Market-Led Strategic Change* (D: 5 pp 159-165 goals and instructions and pp 170-173 diagnostic worksheets.

The purpose of Diagnostic 3 is to open up some understanding of conflicting perceptions about what type of marketing organization exists in your organization (university/college) and how it might be improved.

Task: Conduct a 15 minute interview with a member of your university/college marketing department (or

its equivalent) Use the Diagnostic 3 worksheets to gather information, characterize the existing type of marketing organization and assess its effectiveness in relation to its role and mission. It may be helpful to supply the interviewee with a list of the worksheet questions prior to the interview.

Extension questions:

Interpret your findings in relation to the following:

1.   How successfully does the marketing organization facilitate a practical focus on the *real* problems of making marketing happen in the university or college?

2.   How clear is the role and mission of the marketing department? To what extent do you think that different people in the department have different ideas about what marketing is doing and what it should be doing in the university or college?

3.   How well suited is the existing marketing organization of the university or college to its current marketing strategies? If you think change is needed, how should it be implemented and how would your proposals affect the allocation of work in the marketing department?

Practical exercises:

1.   Read the company scenarios A-D on pages 136-140 in chapter 5 of *Market-Led Strategic Change*. Investigate the causes of 'short-termism', inertia, introspection and lack of customer-orientation in the hospitality and tourism industries. How would you set about inculcating a more innovative, creative and customer-focused approach?

2.   Read 'The case of the disillusioned customers' on pages 144-145 in chapter 9 of *Strategic Hospitality Management*. What can marketing and operations managers do to improve the effectiveness of their customer support? Present your recommendations in the form of a plan for implementing customer support in a national chain of mid-price hotels.

3.   Using the four stage audit approach explained on pages 152-155 in chapter 9 of *Strategic Hospitality Management*, conduct an audit of the food service operations at your university or college. Use your findings to justify establishing (or improving) a supportive internal marketing organization.

3
SERVICES MARKETING

INTRODUCTION

The role of managers in the hospitality/tourism industries often emphasizes the maintenance of appropriate quality and efficiency standards in core products such as food and accommodation. However, the customer in most instances will only be fully satisfied if these components are accompanied by satisfactory levels of service. While the core products will be expected to reach certain standards, it will be the service delivered by personnel and technology that will determine the customer's overall impression of the company and its products.

The extent to which *services marketing* differs from marketing tangible products has been the subject of debate for some time. Some authors make no distinction between the two, while others maintain that there are real differences in approach. A consensus appears to be emerging that whilst services marketing has significant distinctive characteristics the underlying principles remain constant. This chapter outlines the role and importance of services to the economy and the issues which are unique to services marketing.

In this chapter:
- An integrated view of the role of services
  (E: 1 pp 3-17)
- The marketing of services
  (A: 1 pp 3-20; B: 13 pp 220-228)
- The unique characteristics of services
  (A: 1 pp 3-20; B: 13 pp 220-228)
- Managing the service offer
  (B: 13 pp 220-228; D: 2 pp 29-66)

REVIEW

An integrated view of the role of services
(E: 1 pp 3-17)
In western nations, services make an important contribution to economic growth because they offer directly exportable expertise. Tourism in particular, provides a valuable source of invisible export income. There are four features of a modern service economy which have become more prominent in the UK and the USA during the 1980s and 1990s.

They personify the role that services play in the national economy:

- Service businesses support other economic activity such as maintenance and repair services, provision for leisure or support for health and educational needs.

- The economic contribution of services can be measured only in relation to the benefits they bestow, directly and indirectly, on related forms of economic activity.

- Control over patterns of both private and public service activity is increasingly dominated by large, multi-unit and sometimes multi-national organizations.

- Rapid changes in the quality of both products and employment are inherent to service sector development. For products, the competitive nature of modern service markets means that they need to be continually adjusted to changing demand. Competition also sustains a persistent pressure to improve labour productivity and reduce job numbers.

The marketing of services
(A: 1 pp 3-20; B: 13 pp 220-228; E: 1 pp 3-17)
Gershuny and Miles (1) define four service concepts:

- *Service industries* - those firms and employees whose major output is intangible or ephemeral (such as hospitality/tourism services).

- *Service products* - not all necessarily produced by service industries, as some manufacturing firms provide services for customers. A car manufacturer's guarantee is an example.

- *Service occupations* - employees involved in service functions may be employed in any type of business or organization, for instance catering or buildings management.

- *Service functions* - individuals providing unpaid services, such as voluntary work.

While these distinctions are useful, there are other equally valid propositions; Levitt for instance distinguishes between tangibles and intangibles, Christopher *et al* (2) suggest that *"service products are those which produce a series of benefits which cannot be stored."* however, Wyckham *et al* (3) maintain that *"services are not different from products"*.

While there is some disagreement about the precise definition of a 'service', there is broad agreement on the basic differences between a service industry and a product-based industry. The differences relate to the following characteristics:

- Hetereogeneity
- Intangibility
- Inseparability
- Lack of ownership by the buyer
- Low barriers to entry

The unique characteristics of services
(A: 1 pp 3-20; B: 13 pp 220-228)

(a) Hetereogeneity
Services are usually designed around the specific requirements of the customer. For instance, a meal ordered by a customer or a room type specified by a guest. This may apply to some manufactured items such as tailored suits or cars, but it is normally restricted to luxury goods. The unique nature of individual service provision makes standardization more difficult to achieve than in other types of business activity. Further, the absence of standardization can leave the customer with a 'fuzzy' image of the service provided, giving rise to post-purchase dissatisfaction even though the organization may have met its own quality criteria.

Efforts to standardize in the hospitality/tourism industries have increased, partly due to the need to improve productivity and competitiveness. Holiday Inn is long renowned for ensuring consistent levels of service as well as standard facilities such as room size, furnishings, and building layout, but during the 1980s rivals began to challenge by emulating this approach. In the 1990s, the main challenge for hotel companies is to find and exploit unique ways of differentiating their brands while at the same time, improving the standard brand specification in accordance with market position, price and customer expectations.

(b) Intangibility
Pure services lack the tangibility of other products. For instance the customer experience of the service provided by a hotel receptionist should be greater than the sum of the administrative tasks performed by that member of staff. The components of the service product cannot be analyzed as easily as a manufactured good even though there may be service elements included with the latter. For example, a car manufacturer may provide unique warranty arrangements in order to provide added value and product differentiation.

The hospitality/tourism provider should attempt to give tangible clues that will assist the customer to understand the product. These may take the form of photographs in a brochure, or even abstract or unrelated images that convey a clear impression of the type of service experience on offer. This is particularly important as customers have little in the way of tangible evidence to remind them of their patronage, so they seek a relatively clear idea of what to expect prior to making a purchase decision.

(c) Inseparability
Service production and delivery (or consumption) generally occur at or about the same time. This particular aspect of services places a great deal of emphasis upon the individual member of staff dealing with the customer. Customers will negotiate with members of staff, who because they work at the interface between production and consumption have a unique opportunity to sell. For instance, waiting staff should not view themselves purely as order-takers but as front-line sales staff. As management cannot closely supervise or control personal transactions, some companies such as 'My Kinda Town' and 'TGI Friday' provide financial incentives in addition to training, so as to encourage staff to sell and establish an appropriate rapport with the customer.

The customer/staff relationship is the most crucial element in the success of any service operation but other customer relationships are also of great significance. For example distributors such as travel agencies or booking services fulfil an important role in representing the service provider and selling facilities, such as rooms or conference packages. These other organizations often need incentives to encourage committed representation.

(d) Perishability
Services cannot be stocked or held over. For instance hotel rooms left vacant one night do not add to the following night's capacity. This creates problems when demand fluctuates, as expensive capital asset and staff costs must still be met. A variety of tactical policies have been devised by service operators to deal with these issues.

Pricing - differential pricing is often used to discount specific markets at specific times, such as weekend breaks which are often targeted at families. In some circumstances a premium, above normal tariff rates can be charged at periods of excess demand such as Christmas Day. Contribution pricing can be used to cover the variable costs (such as some labour costs, heating and lighting) and make a contribution to the fixed costs of an enterprise.

By way of illustration, some luxury hotels in the west end of London will discount their room rates significantly, late at night when rooms remain unsold.

Promotion - tactical promotions such as sales promotion, direct mail and merchandising can offer significant advantages to hospitality/tourism service operators but should be used carefully in order to avoid a long-term reduction in average spend or change in market positioning. A combination of promotional tools should be used to ensure maximum benefit to the operator. The revenue cost of discount vouchers, perhaps as part of a direct mail policy, may be partially recouped through improved merchandising or personal selling by operatives.

(e) Lack of ownership
The nature of service industry products means that while a customer has temporary use of a facility such as a hotel room, hire car, or restaurant table, they cannot own it. Thus a customer will remain in possession of a number of short term benefits (a good nights sleep, a full stomach) and long term impressions which will influence future recommendations and re-purchase. Lack of ownership may mean that customers are vulnerable to competitive promotions and offers as they have no need to concern themselves with the compatibility of existing products.

Customers are prone to re-interpret their experience either because of competitive promotions or information provided by others. In such circumstances it is difficult to apply notions of 'brand loyalty' to service operations, though many hospitality companies are adapting practices from the fast moving consumer goods (FMCG) sector with some measure of success. One such practice is the maintenance of a customer database to maintain a link with customers, but the use of direct or 'database marketing' is controversial due to its intrusive nature. Specific offers rather than general propositions are regarded as being more effective in building and maintaining customer loyalty. Conventional communication tools like advertising and public relations are also widely used to maintain customer awareness of the service product.

Managing the service offer
(B: 13 pp 220-228; D: 2 pp 29-66)
People are so central to the service product that some authors (4) regard them as an essential part of the service marketing mix (with product, price, promotion and location/distribution). The 'people dimension' gains added significance when the product offering is intangible:

"In product orientated business, the physical reality of the product provides a simple but powerful base on which to build a business description." (5)

"In goods marketing there is a tangible core around which the offering can be developed." (6)

In service industries, people *are* this central core. The impact of the people element is increased because of customer access and expectations. In industrial markets access to operatives is extremely limited. In service markets however access is far greater. The overwhelming majority of staff have some form of direct customer contact, to most customers the hotel receptionist or restaurant waiter represents a major component of the service experience.

The customer/staff relationship presents a significant challenge to the hospitality/tourism manager who must try to achieve company service objectives through a workforce that invariably has a margin of discretion in dealing with customers. The margin of discretion may result in apparently varying service standards and customer dissatisfaction.

Piercy questions the extent to which many organizations are committed to measuring customer satisfaction/dissatisfaction:

"My suspicion is that all to often we do not measure customer satisfaction because we do not want to know the results. Either it is not that important to us, or possibly we are frightened of what the results are going to be...it has to be said that in many cases the real answer is that customer satisfaction is not seen by managers and their organizations as the highest priority in evaluating and planning the business. They say it is, but really it isn't...Quite simply: to make marketing work, customer satisfaction has to be the top priority in all we do..." (D: 2 p. 57).

Management has at its disposal a number of tools such as training, recruitment policy, incentive schemes, sales promotions and so on that can help to regulate service interaction. If in the process of regulation, the hospitality/tourism manager can preserve the unique talents that individuals bring to the workplace, then the company will reap the benefits of a superior service product. In an industry with predominantly low barriers to entry and little legal protection for innovative service ideas, this is an extremely important consideration.

In addition to staffing, key issues for the future of hospitality/tourism services are automation and productivity.

Technology already plays an important role in certain markets such as business, conference and leisure and future advances will enable managers to exercise greater control over manpower costs and service quality issues.

CONCLUSION

The service sector makes an important contribution to the economies of developed countries. Increased leisure time and the growing internationalization of trade means that the contribution made by hospitality and tourism services will continue to grow. For most purposes the principles of marketing have a common application to both service and non-service products although the unique characteristics of services means a difference of approach rather than substance. Controlling the customer/staff relationship, where most of the service offering occurs in hospitality operations, provides an opportunity for product differentiation and competitive advantage. In the future, technological advancements will almost certainly provide the means of enhancing the customer experience through better control of operational variables.

References:

1.   J.I.Gershuny and I.D. Miles. *The New Service Economy.* Frances Pinter, New York, 1983.
2.   M.Christopher, M. McDonald and G. Wills. *Introducing Marketing.* Pan Books, London, 1980.
3.   R.G.Wyckham, T.Fitzroy, G.D. Mandry. 'Marketing Services', *European Journal of Marketing* , 9 (1), 1975.
4.   D.Cowell, *The Marketing of Services.* Butterworth-Heinemann, London, 1991.
5.   D.R.E.Thomas, 'Strategy Is Different in Service Business', *Harvard Business Review,* July-August, 1978.
6.   C.Gronoos, 'A service orientated Approach to the Marketing of Services', *European Journal of Marketing,* 12, (8), 1979.

Review questions:

1.   Identify and compare the *service components* of two fast food operations that you have recently visited. Evaluate the role of the service element, compared to the food and design of the operation, in your overall assessment of the 'meal experience'.

2.   Explain the characteristics of services using the example of a leisure facility that serves a predominantly local market.

3.   Make recommendations for the introduction of technology to improve the level of three star hospitality service to short stay business travellers. Explain how you would communicate the benefits of any changes to your target market.

EXTENSION

Read: either Chapter 4, 'Marketing Strategy and the Marketing Mix in Services Marketing' in D.Cowell, *The Marketing of Services*, Butterworth-Heinemann, London, 1991.

or Chapter 1 of *Hotel and Food Service Marketing* (A: 1 pp 3-20)

The chapter in Cowell (chapter 4) explains a systematic approach to the development of appropriate levels of customer service. Marketing planning and the central role of developing marketing strategy is cited as a part of this systematic process.

Buttle (chapter 1) gives an overview of the service sector and explains some of its characteristics.

Extension questions:

1.   Prepare an *introduction* to a marketing plan for a hospitality/tourism operation of your choice.

2.   Assess the implications for the formulation of an effective promotions policy relating to the issues identified in EQ (1) above.

Practical exercises:

1.   Choose any hospitality/tourism operation in the area and identify the service components of the product.

2.   Propose an outline service statement and marketing plan for the operation as identified in PE (1) above.

4
RESEARCH DESIGN

INTRODUCTION

"Marketing management makes strategic and tactical decisions intended to produce customer and corporate satisfaction. Decisions made in an information vacuum are much more likely to be inadequate - hence the role of marketing research." (B: 3 p. 42.)

Managers rely on accurate information in their role as decision-makers. This means that organizations must ensure that their research processes and information systems are effectively designed and implemented. This chapter examines the issues influencing the design of marketing research programmes in meeting information needs.

In this chapter:
- What is marketing research? (A: 3 pp 42-44; B: 6 pp 106-108)
- Types of marketing research (C: 5 pp 99-100)
- In-house or agency research? (A: 3 pp 45-46; B: 6 pp 108-109; C: 5 pp 101-104)
- The research process (C: 5 pp 104-105)
- Limitations of marketing research (C: 5 p. 105)

REVIEW

What is marketing research?
(A: 3 pp 42-44; B: 6 pp 106-108)
Marketing research can be defined as:
"The systematic and objective search for and analysis of information relevant to the identification and solution of any problem in the field of marketing." (1).

Marketing research is systematic if it is planned and if it follows a sequence of logically-ordered steps, from problem definition to problem solution. Further, its reliability depends on the design of the research programme and the way in which methods and techniques for observation, data collection and analysis are used. Providing criteria for ensuring objectivity and reliability are established and met, any type of marketing activity can be investigated and analyzed.

It is important to note here the differences between market research and marketing research.

While *market research* aims to describe markets - their size, location and pattern of development, *marketing research* is much wider in its application to marketing problems.

A number of factors influenced the developing role of market and marketing research:

- *The size of firms* - as size increases, the distance between marketing decision-makers, customers and suppliers is also likely to increase.

- *Market scope* - costs and risks increase as a firm's focus shifts from local to national and even international markets.

- *The need for information* - a commitment to systematic research is required in order to monitor customer needs and identify market trends in a meaningful way.

- *Unpredictable market forces* - the need to continually monitor the impact of change on society, lifestyles, expectations and how these affect customer choice, especially how non-price variables influence behaviour.

These factors, among others, place a premium on information for effective marketing decision-making. They also justify experimentation with data gathering and the development of new approaches for systemizing research.

Types of marketing research (C: 5 pp 99-100)
The main types of marketing research are:

(a) Market and sales research
Including: estimates of market size for both developed and new markets; the identification of market characteristics and segments; the identification of market trends; sales forecasting; obtaining information on customers and potential customers and obtaining information on competitors.

(b) Product research
Including: the generation of new product ideas; product concept testing; product trials; the test marketing of products; the investigation of different packaging types and alternatives.

(c) Pricing research
Is concerned with the relationships between product/service pricing and demand.

(d) Marketing communications research
Covers: the effectiveness of marketing communications; media selection research; copy testing and sales territory planning.

(e) Distribution research
Covers: warehouse location research and retail outlet location research.

In-house or agency research?
(A: 3 pp 45-46; B: 6 pp 108-109; C: 5 pp 101-104)
The ideal approach to marketing research is for a firm to develop its own programmes, but this is not always a viable option due to the costs involved. In fact, a well-organized marketing research department or team with a qualified manager and trained staff is costly. It is therefore important to differentiate between frequent and infrequent information needs so that a programme of internal (or in-house) marketing research can be tailored to organizational priorities. Buttle illustrates this (Table 3.2, A: 3 p. 46) by distinguishing between the frequency of information needed for a variety of hospitality marketing decisions. He uses two categories for this purpose:

(a) Recurrent hospitality marketing problems requiring continuous information inputs:
These might include: regular appraisal of salespersons' performance; analysis of actual sales of accommodation and food and beverage against forecast sales; tracking of seasonal patterns in sales; setting monthly sales targets for regional sales offices; monitoring actual promotional expenditure against budget; considering whether to match changes in competitors' bar prices.

(b) Occasional hospitality marketing problems requiring ad hoc information inputs:
These might include: whether to co-operate with adjacent hotels in joint promotions; whether to sponsor a sporting event; whether to launch a new food and beverage format; whether to close a floor of bedrooms during the winter period; to discover the reasons for poor sales performance from a particular office; to see if profitable opportunities exist for franchising a restaurant outlet.

Additionally, it is desirable from time to time to undertake broader-based programmes of research to assess the forces affecting change in the marketplace. For this reason, most organizations commission marketing research agencies to undertake occasional programmes of research. Agencies often specialize in particular types of research using customized data collection and analytical techniques and appropriately trained personnel. This combination can provide impartial and in-depth practical experience on specific projects, but it is clearly important to ensure that the agency fully understands the client's products and information needs. There are a number of factors to consider when deciding whether to conduct research programmes in-house or employ an agency:

- *Cost.* It is often cheaper to use internal, suitably qualified and experienced personnel. It is however, important to balance this consideration against other internal priorities. Procedures for conducting research are normally time-consuming and there may be other types of project work which can be conducted more quickly and easily by members of the marketing team.
- *Research expertise.* It is important to consider whether or not the necessary expertise is available internally, especially when sophisticated research techniques are needed.
- *Product or service knowledge.* Research requiring in-depth technical knowledge might be better suited to an in-house team, especially if a product-specific interpretation of research needs and findings is necessary.
- *Objectivity.* External agencies can often be more objective, especially if the in-house team is too familiar or too close to the research project brief.
- *Special equipment.* Depending upon the nature of the inquiry, it may be that the research calls for specialist computer programs or test equipment which an agency can provide.
- *Confidentiality.* In the UK, the Market Research Society and Industrial Marketing Association among others, regulate member agencies and organizations by means of codes of conduct. The confidentiality of research is an important issue, especially if it relates to new product or service development and testing. If particular types of research are deemed sensitive, it may be easier to undertake the research in-house, unless confidentiality and the security of findings can be assured.

The research process (C: 5 pp 104-105)
A decision to conduct research must take into account the value of the information to be obtained. In fact, research should only be conducted when it is expected that the value of information will be greater than the cost of obtaining it. The research process begins after this decision has been taken and it consists of a series of nine steps:

(a) Define the problem
What is the marketing problem? How can it be resolved? Interpreting these issues, what are the most appropriate research objectives?

(b) Select the data collection method(s)
In marketing research there are two principal categories of data - primary and secondary research. Primary data are collected to solve the specific

problem at hand. The most commonly used data collection methods include: survey research, personal interviews, observational research and experimentation. Secondary data are collected mainly for background purposes rather than to resolve the specific problem under consideration.

(c) Select the sampling method(s)
In some circumstances it may not be necessary to select a sample if all or most of the population in question can be approached. For example, a project designed to assess distributor reactions to a new marketing policy could be undertaken by obtaining the reactions of all distributors. Conversely, a project designed to assess customer reactions to a new product idea may need to be carefully targeted by means of the sample selection.

(d) Specify the research design and plan
This step involves specifying the data collection method(s), the sample and data to be collected, how it will be analyzed (including the analytical procedures to be employed) and the way in which results will be reported and summarized.

(e) Estimate the time and resources needed
This step encompasses timings, costs, resources (such as people and equipment) and any other considerations which may affect the successful completion of the work.

(f) Obtain approval for the research project
This usually involves presenting the research plan as defined by steps *(a-e)* to the committee or individual(s) with the authority to approve the project.

(g) Undertake data collection
This requires working to a carefully written plan for implementing and research, with particular reference to arrangements for monitoring and controlling field work.

(h) Undertake data analysis
Prior to analysis, data has to be coded and in the case of non-questionnaire data, interpreted. At this stage, it is important to run checks for missing data and for the reliability and consistency of the coding work undertaken.

(i) Write the research report
The report contains a summary of the research findings and the implications which arise. A balanced interpretation should take into account sources of inaccuracy and/or ambiguity in the data set.

Limitations of marketing research (C: 5 p. 105)
As many aspects of marketing research are behaviourally-based it is difficult to anticipate and/or eliminate every possible source of error. It should be noted however, that the procedures used to specify the research design and plan should take account of the following potential sources of error:

- *Sampling error*. These are errors in the specification of the target population and/or errors caused by the selection of a non-representative sample.
- *Non-response errors*. Include a failure to contact all members of a sample and/or failure by such members to respond to the research effort.
- *Data collection errors*. Include the possibility that respondents in some situations may provide answers to please, impress or irritate the interviewer. Data collection errors can also be caused by leading questions, and here it is the fault of the questionnaire designer, in that the way the question is worded may lead the respondent to give a wrong response. To avoid this, questionnaires as well as other data collection methods should be piloted prior to use. Other potential sources of error include incorrectly recorded answers due to misinterpretation or carelessness by research team members.
- *Analytical and reporting errors*. These are caused by using inappropriate procedures to analyze the data or by an incorrect interpretation of the findings.
- *Experimental errors*. Experiments are designed to measure the impact of one variable (e.g. advertising) on another (e.g. sales). Experimental error may arise if uncontrollable events occur during the experiment (e.g. if a competitor launches a new product during a test period).

Despite the importance of primary data for decision-making, it is important to analyze and use existing information wherever this is possible, prior to initiating an expensive data collection exercise. In doing so, it may obviate the need for data collection or help to clarify new information needs more precisely.

CONCLUSION

The collection, analysis, and dissemination of information is increasingly a key element in a firm's domestic and international success. Managers cannot make sound business decisions without reliable data. A host of decisions depends on such data - which national markets to enter, what national strategies and plans to pursue, what price to charge, and what distribution channels to use. (2).

The fundamental role of marketing research is to reduce the level of uncertainty and help decision-makers to make the best managerial choice. By collecting and analyzing information in a systematic and objective way, marketing research can help to identify and resolve many of the problems which organizations face.

Marketing research encompasses a broader perspective than market research because it is concerned with broad-based issues like sales, pricing, communications and distribution and it may be carried out in-house or by an agency. The decision to use an agency must be carefully weighed because of the prices charged and the type and sensitivity of the information involved.

Due to the nature of behaviourally based business activity, marketing research is not immune from sources of error, namely: sampling error, non-response error, data collection errors, analytic and reporting errors, and experimental errors. However, the occurrence of these errors can be minimized during the research design phase.

References:

1.   P.E.Green and D.S.Tull. *Research for Marketing Decisions*. Prentice-Hall, Englewood Cliffs, NJ, 4th Edition, 1987.
2.   B.Toyne and P.Walters. *Global Marketing Management: A Strategic Perspective*. Allyn and Bacon, Needham Heights, MA. 2nd Edition, 1993.

Review questions:

1.   Identify the differences between *market research* and *marketing research* and list the areas of study covered by each of them.

2.   A number of factors have influenced the importance of market and marketing research. Explain how these factors interact so as to place a premium on information for marketing decisions.

3.   Prior to carrying out marketing research it is desirable to calculate the value of the information to be obtained. Identify and discuss the factors affecting this decision.

4.   Identify and explain the factors that need to be considered when devising the research design and plan needed to evaluate a foreign market opportunity.

EXTENSION

Read: 'A Multivariate Approach Towards Marketing Decisions in the Convention Segment.' by W.J.Quain, B.Render and P.W.Hermann, *International Journal of Hospitality Management*, Vol. 10, No 2, 1991, pp 147-155.

This article presents a study carried-out for the purpose of determining the most important type of advertising medium used by travellers in selecting a hotel. It discusses the differences in using advertising for hotel selection between market segments, particularly the convention segment.

Note: If this article is not available in your library, select an alternative article to use in conjunction with the questions below.

Extension questions:

1.   What type of data does marketing research provide and how may these data be used?

2.   If your main competitor launches a new product, what kind of marketing research should you undertake to assess its impact? What research techniques would you use?

3.   What special conditions apply when conducting a marketing research programme at a foreign destination? How would you modify the programme to take account of them?

Practical exercises:

1.   Discuss the importance of marketing research to the hospitality/tourism industries and devise a list of questions for testing the suitability and validity of research design proposals.

2.   As the marketing director of a hospitality /tourism firm you have decided to contract an agency to carry out a study relating to the development of a new product. What criteria should be used to select and assess the agency?

3.   A foreign company has just acquired your main hospitality/tourism competitor. Using a desk research approach, draw-up a list of information sources to assess the possible changes in your competitor's strategy.

4.   Observe the behaviour of selected restaurant or pub customers and from your analysis, identify how aspects of the product presentation could be improved.

5
DATA COLLECTION

INTRODUCTION

"Market research is one of management's most useful tools, but only when it is properly performed, interpreted, and acted upon. It provides executives with solid knowledge about their markets, allowing them to understand customers' preferences, perceptions, and motivations. Such insights are especially important when consumers and competitive offerings are changing as rapidly as they are today." (1)

To be successful in the marketplace, an organization must carefully analyze its business environment by collecting data on business patterns and trends and the opportunities posed by them. This chapter seeks to outline the various types and sources of information available and to explore some of the main data collection methods used in marketing.

In this chapter:
- Marketing research data (A: 3 pp 49-52)
- Secondary sources (B: 6 pp 111-115)
- Primary research (B: 6 pp 115-116; C: 5 p. 109)
- Survey research (A: 3 pp 56-65; B: 6 pp 118-119; C: 5 pp 109-118)
- Personal interviews (C: 5 pp 118-119)
- Observational research (B: 6 p. 120; C: 5 p. 120)
- Experimentation (B: 6 pp 119-120; C: 5 pp 120-121)

REVIEW

Marketing research data (A: 3 pp 49-52)
As noted in chapter 4, information is vital to effective marketing and, having decided what type of information is needed, the next step is to locate and access it.

An important aspect of data collection is the availability, accessibility and reliability of data: *"It is normally cheaper to look for and use information that has already been collected (secondary information) than it is to collect new information. If fortunate, the user may find that secondary information is sufficiently pertinent, accurate, timely and usable. Secondary information is normally cheaper and quicker because it involves less search time, little or no fieldwork (interviewing),*

or data analysis. Secondary information may be internal or external to the organization." (A: 3 p. 49)

Secondary sources (B: 6 pp 111-115)
Secondary information sources are the logical starting point for most planning and research projects. Secondary information is: *"...data neither collected directly by the user nor specifically for the user..."* (B p. 111) and the collection activity is often termed 'desk research'. This is a broadly defined term encompassing among others, the collection and analysis of published material, information from internal sources, salespersons and external sources such as customers and suppliers.

There are many internal information sources spanning strategic, specialist and operational functions. The major sources of quantifiable data include:
- *Production* - output, inventory, costs, productivity and utilization.

- *Distribution* - goods in transit, stock levels and locations, stock turn rates and absolute throughput.

- *Purchasing* - costs, rate of change of costs, materials, sources.

- *Sales* - distribution and location of accounts, value and volume of trade, major developments.

- *Marketing services* - expenditure, forecasts of turnover or likely developments.

- *Finance* - costs, depreciation, overheads and other ratios.

- *Personnel* - staff and wage costs, trends, shortages and efficiency levels.

This information can be augmented by other industry statistics collected and distributed by trade associations, industry research associations and, in specific contexts, by chambers of commerce and development agencies.

Primary research (B: 6 pp 115-116; C: 5 p. 109)
When information from secondary sources is insufficient or inadequate, the next step is to collect primary data. This is information gathered by direct contact with consuming, buying, intermediary or influencing groups. There are numerous ways of collecting primary research data, including: personally administered and postal questionnaires, personal and telephone interviews, participant observation, and experimentation.

Survey research (A: 3 pp 56- 65; B: 6 pp 118-119; C: 5 pp 109-118)

"(A survey involves) a technique in which members of the population of interest are interviewed. If all members are surveyed, it becomes a census; if only a portion, it is a sample survey. (A: 3 p. 56).

If it is to be effective as a means of collecting information accurately and systematically, the design of a survey requires careful planning. Design and testing should follow a four-stage sequence: (a) preparation; (b) preliminary decisions (c) piloting and (d) refining.

(a) Preparation

The first priority is to set the survey research objectives and define as precisely as possible what information is needed to meet them.

(b) Preliminary decisions

The next step is to review secondary information sources in order to establish the contribution of prior work and to identify constraints or barriers which may arise. In some circumstances data may be difficult to obtain and/or verify, and it is helpful to identify potential barriers to data collection beforehand. Following this, the sample can be defined by analyzing the target population, deciding on the appropriate sample size and sampling method and the most suitable means of communication. The most frequently used methods of data collection are by postal questionnaire, telephone interview, or personal interview.

A postal survey is a cost-effective way of collecting responses from a geographically dispersed population. Further, it is well suited to large samples because it is faster and cheaper than personal interviewing, and almost as quick as telephone interviewing. Telephone interviewing can be useful when time is short, but it is important to bear in mind its costs, and the timing of calls. A personal interview format is particularly well suited to the exploration of situations and events where the respondent's reaction and interpretation is sought. Further, it is a useful way of pre-testing topic areas and questions prior to finalizing the design of a self-completion questionnaire, which must contain clear, unambiguous questions to ensure the best possible rate of response.

(c) Piloting

It is important to pre-test or pilot survey instruments like questionnaires and personal interview schedules to check for clarity of meaning and ease of use. The context in which the data will be collected and the topic areas addressed should also be carefully monitored during piloting.

A questionnaire is typically used to collect an array of data relating to a respondent's behaviour, demographic profile, level of knowledge, attitudes, interests and opinions. It is therefore particularly important to assess levels of respondent sensitivity to questions dealing with personal and or sensitive issues. If reactions are negative to one or more questions of this type, it will be necessary to re-formulate or omit them so that the chances of respondents completing and returning the questionnaire are not diminished.

There are some basic rules for good questionnaire design - ideally it should be simple, short, and easily understood. It is important to keep in mind what kind of information is needed, who can provide the information, and the best way of collecting it. There are numerous published sets of guidelines that can be used to assist with the design and layout of a questionnaire and to help ensure that it follows a logical format. The following guidelines (C: 5 pp 111-112) exemplify this.

- The overall questionnaire should move from topic to topic in a logical manner, with all questions on one topic completed before moving to the next.

- Sensitive questions, such as the respondent's income should be at the end.

- The first few questions should be simple, objective and interesting.

- The questionnaire should be designed so as to minimize recording errors and assist analysis.

- The questionnaire should be pre-tested with respondents similar to those who will be included in the final survey.

There are several different types of questions used in questionnaires: direct questions, indirect questions and attitude questions. Direct questions can be sub-divided into open and closed questions. Open questions allow respondents to answer in their own words. Closed questions include all possible answers, and the respondents choose from among them. Closed questions can also be dichotomous (allow only two responses such as 'yes-no', 'agree-disagree' often supplemented by a third neutral category such as 'don't know') or multiple-choice (allowing three or more responses).

- *Direct questions* should be open, but in the case of closed-dichotomous or closed-multiple-choice, it depends on the specific purpose of the questionnaire, as each has its advantages and disadvantages.

In answering open questions, the respondent is not guided by optional statements, which is an advantage, but at the same time he/she might experience difficulties in articulating a suitable response and the variability of answers given can constitute a disadvantage.

On the other hand, closed questions are easier for the respondent and interviewer and they aid questionnaire analysis, but they require careful preparation and pre-testing to ensure that they fully reflect the question scenario. To make best use of open and closed question formats, researchers often use open questions in preliminary research situations and with feed-back from this stage it is then possible to formulate closed questions for pre-testing and survey use.

- *Indirect questions* are used when it is not possible to obtain the information through direct questioning. This can happen if the topic area is considered to be embarrassing or controversial.

- *Attitude questions* are used to explore underlying beliefs and to help predict or interpret behavioural patterns. Attitude data can be collected using direct or indirect questions.

(d) Refining
This constitutes the final step in the design of the survey instrument and in the case of a questionnaire, refinements to questions and adjustments to the layout take place after pre-testing under field conditions. Pre-testing is usually undertaken by piloting the questionnaire with a small number of representative respondents.

Finally, it is important to carefully monitor the response rate in order to assure the validity of the research. It is difficult to avoid some level of non-response, particularly in mail or telephone surveys, but there are several ways of minimizing lower levels of response rate. This can be done by choosing the subject matter carefully, communicating with the respondent before sending the questionnaire, by offering token incentives to reply, and by sending reminder letters.

Personal interviews (C: 5 pp 118-119)
If there is the need to conduct a series of interviews, these must be well prepared during the desk research stage, because it is important to acquire a knowledge of the background to the discussions that will take place in the field. It is also important to conduct a series of pilot interviews before starting the main programme to check that the schedule of questions is adequate for the purposes of the investigation and appropriately structured.

The format and approach to personal interviewing largely depends on the situation and context. A programme of research relating to an industrial market may require personal interviews with personnel at all organizational levels and the interviewer will need sufficient confidence and skill to vary the format, language and approach taken. Conversely, interviews held with customers are generally more uniform and because of this, a more structured approach can be used to ensure consistency of treatment. In both cases however, interviewers need to be good communicators and sufficiently skilled to be able to manage an array of interpersonal situations including interviewees who are uncommunicative, suspicious or even hostile.

Observational research (B: 6 pp 120; C: 5 pp 120)
Participant observation is extensively used in the social sciences. The main purpose is to observe the behaviour of people in controlled or actual situations so as to gain insights into their reactions. It is often easier and more natural for the researcher to participate in the same activity and/or interact with the people under observation.For example, this is would be an appropriate way to assess customer reactions to a restaurant or pub environment. Other variations include direct observation (examining how people behave in specific situations) and observation recording (using electromechanical devices for monitoring respondents' reactions).

"The real value of observational studies lies in their ability to describe routines and patterns of behaviour. The nature of the approach calls for the researcher to infer causality if that is sought by the study." (B: 6 p. 120).

Experimentation
(B: 6 pp 119-120; C: 5 pp 120-121)
"Experimentation involves the manipulation of one or more variables by the experimenter in such a way that its effect on another variable can be determined, e.g. manipulating price in order that its effect on sale can be determined." (C: 5 p. 120).

Experimentation is more widely used in the natural sciences because its use in social science settings is restricted by the difficulties of setting-up and verifying experimental situations. However, experimentation in a marketing context is especially appropriate to the testing of new products. It can also be used in a broader context to test for changes in controlled market situations. In this instance, marketing mix variables are manipulated in order to identify the optimal relationships between the marketing mix and marketing strategy.

CONCLUSION

Data collection is essential to the supply of marketing information for decision-making and planning. Desk research provides the background to primary research and careful preparation helps to ensure a sound, well structured approach. In most cases, marketing research is undertaken using survey methods although observation and experimentation might be used in specific circumstances.

Preparation, design, piloting and refinement are important steps in survey research as the procedures for data collection and the sources used must be carefully specified, tested and verified to ensure that they coincide with the objectives that have been set. A similar sequence applies to the testing of specific data collection instruments such as questionnaires and question schedules for use in personal interviewing. Pre-testing helps to ensure that ambiguities and sources of inconsistency are identified and the instruments can then be refined prior to use. In all cases, pre-testing should be based upon a representative sample drawn from the target population. In this way it is possible to ensure that data collection is properly focused and the issues that may impede data collection have been identified and addressed before the programme of research commences.

Reference:

1.   *The Marketing Strategy Portfolio.* Strategic Direction Publishers Ltd., Volume 1, Zurich, 1993.

Review questions:

1.   Identify the differences between *secondary data* and *primary data,* and explain in what contexts each should be used.

2.   Why is it important to pilot a questionnaire and how should it be done?

3.   What are the main issues influencing questionnaire design?

EXTENSION

Read: 'Quality in the Hospitality Industry: A Study.' by M.P.Coyle and B.G.Dale, *International Journal of Hospitality Management*, Vol. 12, No. 2, 1993, pp 141-153.

The article presents a study of the determinants of quality from both customer and provider viewpoints, across a range of hospitality providers. The study identifies a number of the gaps which exist between the perceptions of customers and providers and shows that in this particular topic area, traditional data collection methods such as questionnaires are inadequate for the purpose of revealing customer expectations of quality of service.

Note: If this article is not available in your library, select an alternative article to use in conjunction with the questions below.

Extension questions:

1.   Market research is not the same as marketing research. What is the relationship between them, and what are the main differences?

2.   What types of survey methods are you familiar with, and in what circumstances would you use each of them?

3.   What criteria would you use to evaluate the value of data collected and analyzed on your behalf by a marketing research company?

4.   Quality of service is sometimes difficult to measure because customers and providers have different expectations and perspectives. Explain how you would collect and verify data which could be used to close this gap.

Practical exercises:

1.   Questionnaires need to be constructed with care since they can contain sources of error. Design a questionnaire to identify the degree of satisfaction of customers with the room service delivered by a hotel.

2.   Marketing researchers investigate the marketing environment and the marketing mix. What kind of information do they get from each of these areas and how should it relate to marketing decision-making?

3.   What applications can you find for observation and experimentation techniques in hospitality /tourism settings? Illustrate your answer by explaining *how* you apply them.

6

DATA ANALYSIS

INTRODUCTION

"Globalization/localization demands a far more sophisticated approach to market research. Cross-border studies are still at an early stage and are hindered by the different and often incompatible methodologies used in individual countries. As companies move towards a more centralized approach to their marketing strategies, they will want a co-ordinated and consistent way of gathering information about products, consumers and competitors and of tracking the effectiveness of promotional tactics. They will want this served up not as an indigestible lump of raw data, but as targeted, value-added analysis." (1).

After collecting the data the next step is to analyze it. The purpose of analysis is to provide meaning - otherwise data will have no sense, form or understandable structure. The analysis of data is of the utmost importance, as it is here that the analyst seeks to interpret the data collected. The analysis can be used by the marketing department and disseminated to other departments to facilitate good communications and closer co-operation in meeting organizational objectives.

In this chapter:
- Analyzing the information
  (A: 3 p. 70; C: 5 p. 124)
- Using the information (A: 3 p. 71)
- Application of research techniques
  (C: 5 pp 128-136)
- Marketing information systems
  (B: 6 pp 124; C:5 pp 136)
- Research reports (C: 5 pp 127-128)

REVIEW

Analyzing the information
(A: 3 pp 70; C: 5 pp 124)
There are numerous techniques for data analysis and they can be classified as univariate, bivariate or multivariate (A: 3 p. 70):

- *Univariate techniques* - analyze data relating to a single variable such as sales, coupon response rates, or customer complaints.

- *Bivariate techniques* - analyze data relating to two variables and look to establish relationships such as correlation or time-order between them. Such studies would include price-sales relationships and salespersons' responses to financial incentives.

- *Multivariate analysis* - the most sophisticated set of techniques, seeks to establish relationships of a causal or correlative nature between at least three variables. Marketing simulations, in which the combined interactive effects of marketing mix decisions on sales and profitability are computed electronically, are a highly developed form of multivariate modelling.

Marketing research analysis usually involves simple tabulation, calculation of frequencies and summary statistics and cross-tabulation.

- *Sampling tabulation* - consists of calculating the number and percentage of respondents who choose each of the available answers.

- *Summarizing statistics* - consists of two kinds of techniques: measures of central tendency and measures of dispersion. The first provides measures of the mid-point of the distribution, and the second gives an indication of the amount of variation in the data comprising the distribution. The major measures of central tendency are the mean, the mode, and the median (2).

- *Cross-tabulation* - involves constructing a table so that responses to two or more questions can be compared. This can be produced by using a statistical program such as SPSS for Windows.

Using the information (A:3 p. 71)
As previously noted, marketing research is an important source of information for managerial decision-making. Managers need to decide between the alternatives available, and in so doing, they must take into account the validity and reliability of the findings. The potential sources of invalidity are: (a) respondent error; (b) investigator error; (c) sampling error and selection effects; (d) history effects; (e) maturity effects; (f) testing effects; (g) instrument effects and most of these sources can be eliminated by careful pre-testing prior to data collection.

Reliability, the most desirable outcome of data collection, is reflected by the level of accuracy and consistency in the data set. If two surveys of the same population provide the same or similar results, then it is reasonable to assume that the findings are reliable. Also, findings are valid if the research instrument used to collect the data actually measures what it is intended to measure. In these circumstances the issue of interpretation is comparatively straightforward and marketing decisions can be made with confidence.

Application of research techniques
(C:5 pp 128-136)
Data analysis can help to inform an array of marketing decisions. These include all the functions of the marketing mix, namely, (a) product research; (b) pricing research; (c) marketing communications research; (d) distribution research; (e) test marketing; and (f) motivation research.

(a) Product research encompasses the following:

- *Generating new products ideas.* Sources of new product ideas include monitoring secondary sources (particularly trade journals), group discussions with customers and/or industry 'experts', studies of product use and surveys of customer requirements.

- *Product concept testing.* A product concept is an idea that has been defined in terms of its applications and benefits. Before developing a new product it is advisable to research the demand for the concept type. The concept is described to a target group of customers with a view to establishing whether they would buy it if it were available.

- *Product testing.* In this test, a target group of customers are asked to use or examine product prototypes, to give their opinions of the tested product and to say if they would buy such a product if available.

- *Test marketing.* A product is tested in a limited geographical area to explore issues such as the best way to launch it, how well it would be received and its relative probability of success in the marketplace.

- *Packaging research.* Packaging is tested in laboratory and field experimentation.

(b) Pricing research relates to the setting of prices for existing and new products and involves forecasting sales and estimating costs. The estimation of costs is sometimes viewed as an accounting function but pricing is often a tactical issue whereby prices are manipulated in the short term to fight a tactical battle, or over a longer term to support product positioning objectives. In circumstances such as these, the marketing

department must be able and willing to conduct or participate in pricing research so that the factors affecting cost dynamics and related pricing options are clearly understood.

(c) Marketing communications research includes:

- *Marketing communications effectiveness research.* Here, the communication and/or sales effect is measured by scrutinizing advertising, personal selling, sales promotion and public relations activity. An assessment of effectiveness is principally concerned with measuring levels of awareness, attitudes and the probability of an 'intention to buy' decision prior to and after a campaign. Relative sales effectiveness can also be assessed by analyzing the relationship between promotional expenditure and sales revenue. If it is to be accurate, a review of sales effectiveness must also examine the sales mix to see how many new sales have been generated during the review period.

- *Media selection research.* The purpose is to select suitable media outlets for product advertising. This entails the collection of data relating to media distribution, audience size, audience exposure, and cost per insertion.

- *Copy testing.* This is concerned with an assessment of the creative dimension of advertising and promotional material. Creative ideas can be evaluated using surveys of advertising recall, focus group discussions and by field and laboratory tests using physiological and psychological techniques to record reactions to different types of creative ideas as well as subtle variations on specific ideas.

- *Researching the number and location of sales representatives required.* In order to assess the effectiveness of regional or local sales representation it is necessary to examine the trends in sales data including contacts made and the conversion of contacts to sales. It is also helpful to undertake a periodic review of the sales effort approach to assess the effectiveness of sales organization, support, training and other resource and personnel issues.

(d) Distribution research is mainly concerned with:

- *Warehouse location research.* This generally involves an assessment of the geographical dispersal of customers, taking into account regional concentrations, distribution costs and foreseeable logistical problems. Other important factors include the availability and cost of warehouse space, its accessibility and suitability.

- *Retail outlet location research.* Above all, customer-related issues must be fully researched and considered. Is the proposed site easily accessible? Are there sufficient potential customers in the catchment area? How successfully will the outlet be able to cope with existing and future competition? If these and other customer-related requirements are met, issues relating to site development and running costs, distribution access and other support costs must be resolved.

(e) Test marketing is used to assess the sales potential and probability of acceptance by customers of a new product or product extension. The test item is offered for sale in one or more selected outlets in one or more localities or regions, and its reception by customers is observed, recorded and analyzed throughout the test period. In this way, test marketing provides supporting data for refining or tuning the product itself and the way in which it is presented and promoted to customers. It also helps to indicate sales potential and the marketing effort required to establish it in the marketplace.

(f) Motivation research seeks to investigate underlying purchase motives and other behavioural influences which are unknown, hidden or too complex to be determined by direct questioning. By gauging subconscious feelings and reactions to a product, related implications for design, packaging, pricing and advertising can be identified.

Marketing information systems
(B: 6 pp 124; C: 5 p. 136)
The existence of information in a company is not enough. It must be structured and disseminated in such a way that it is possible for managers to use it to formulate policies, make decisions and resolve problems. While marketing research is concerned with generating information, the marketing information system is focused on managing the flow of information.

The collection, analysis and dissemination of data is increasingly viewed as an integral part of the on-going need to build and sustain a marketing information system (B: 6 p. 124). The development of such a system calls for a careful study of both the information needs of the company and its managers and employees and the methods and resources needed to acquire the information.

In some organizations, marketing information is viewed as a component part of its management

information system (C: 5 p. 137), together with other sub-systems:

- *Internal accounting* - a system that reports orders, sales, inventory levels, receivables and payables.
- *Environmental scanning* - the set of procedures and sources used by executives to obtain their everyday information about trends and developments in the business environment.
- *Research, development and planning* - the systematic design, collection, analysis and reporting of data and findings relevant to product and market options and opportunities.

Research reports (C: 5 pp 127-128)
The final stage of a research project is to communicate the results. This can be done in written or oral format, or both. To ensure that findings and recommendations are presented as clearly as possible, it is important to ensure that presentation materials are sequenced in a logical and helpful way. In producing written reports, it is normal practice to use guidelines so that the layout and style of the documentation is consistent and appropriate to the intended readership.

Report guidelines normally include notes on the sequencing of material, how it should be presented (use of headings, subheadings and section numbering) the role of appendices in summarizing research design, results and other technical details and the style of writing needed to communicate in the most appropriate way with the intended readership. Some of these points are illustrated in the following guideline notes (C: 5 p. 128):

- The report sequence is usually title page, table of contents, summary, introduction/research objectives, research methodology, findings, conclusions, recommendations (if appropriate), appendices.
- Most report readers will not be particularly concerned with the technical aspects of the report such as sampling procedure and questionnaire design. For this reason technical details should be placed in the appendix section rather than in the methodology section.
- Use terminology that matches the vocabulary of the reader.
- Use diagrams (such as graphs, bar charts and pie charts) whenever possible.
- If results are to be communicated orally, the presentation sequence is normally research objectives, research methodology, major findings, conclusions and recommendations. In this format of presentation, visual aids play an important role in maintaining audience attention.

CONCLUSION

The success of research depends on the approach taken and on the importance attached to ensuring that it is properly conceived and resourced. There are several key implications for organizations either conducting or commissioning research:

- Build up a long term relationship with a research supplier, rather than working on an ad hoc, project-by-project basis.
- Aim to conduct research *before* marketing decisions are taken rather than using it to justify marketing action.
- Use existing customer information sources wherever possible as a means of guiding and verifying segmentation research.
- Don't allow information overload to occur or marketing decisions to be taken in circumstances which may have become confused by conflicting research data. (1)

Data analysis plays a vital role in marketing decision-making. The way in which customer and market behaviour are interpreted is fundamental to identifying ways of sustaining competitive success. A systematic approach to research and to disseminating marketing information (see also chapter 13) will help to ensure that the marketing department remains sensitive to customer needs and can discern changes quickly and effectively.

References:

1. The Economist Intelligence Unit. *Marketing 2000: Critical Challenges for Corporate Survival*. EIU Management Guide, London, 1991.

2. L.W.Rodger. *Statistics for Marketing*. McGraw-Hill, London, 1984, pp 179-186.

Review questions:

1. Using hospitality/tourism examples, differentiate between and explain the uses and applications of qualitative and quantitative analytical techniques.

2. What are the main sources of invalidity in primary research? Explain with reference to a research plan for a hospitality/tourism project how you would attempt to prevent or minimize sources of invalidity.

3. Explain how marketing research could be used to optimize the marketing mix in a hospitality /tourism organization of your choice.

EXTENSION

Read: 'Patron Preferences for Features Offered by Licensed Clubs.' by A.O.Bull and K.M.Alcock, *International Journal of Contemporary Hospitality Management*, Vol. 5, No. 1, 1993, pp 28-32.

During the 1980s and early 1990s many new leisure and recreational products were introduced, especially in home entertainment. To stay profitable, Australian clubs, with their multi-attribute products, have had to tailor their products more precisely to the needs of patrons in the same way as other hospitality businesses. This article explains and illustrates the use of conjoint analysis to examine the benefits perceived by patrons at two popular Australian clubs.

Note: If this article is not available in your library, select an alternative article to use in conjunction with the questions below.

Extension questions:

1. Suggest how sources of invalidity may affect the validity and reliability of research findings.

2. Explain how research techniques could be used to generate and test new hospitality /tourism product ideas.

3. Discuss the importance of media selection research for hospitality/tourism advertising.

Practical exercises:

1. Select a holiday product from a tour operator and set up a pilot product test. Report on findings and recommendations.

2. Compare the research needs of two hospitality/tourism organizations (one large and one small). Present your findings in the form of a research plan proposal for each organization.

3. A basic distinction between data analysis techniques can be made according to the number of variables analyzed - univariate, bivariate or multivariate. Try to find one or more examples of each type of analysis by scanning the reports held in your library. Prepare a critique of the reports and use examples to illustrate what you consider to be good and bad examples of data presentation and report writing.

7
PLANNING

INTRODUCTION

"In the '90s, the battle for market share will become an all-out war...Every hotel and lodging company must become more market driven, improving their product, improving their service and examining their price in an effort to create a unique, sustainable, competitive advantage in the local marketplace and a perception of greater value for their guests."
(F: 5 p. 72.)

Planning is a business process which encompasses an appraisal of what has been achieved in the recent past, a debate about how improvements can be made for the future and how they can be achieved. Specifically, marketing planning seeks to identify the ingredients of sustainable competitive success. It encompasses marketing information, strategies (on issues such as segmentation, differentiation and positioning), programmes of marketing action and procedures for evaluating outcomes. The aim of this chapter is to examine the ingredients of marketing planning and the issues relating to its successful implementation.

In this chapter:
- The marketing plan (D: 7 pp 242-244)
- The planning hierarchy (D: 4 pp 117-120; A: 6 pp 137-158)
- An overview of the planning process (B: 27 pp 416-430; D: 7 pp 235-245 and 256-264)
- Barriers to effective marketing planning (D: 4 pp 117-120; D 6: 247-249)
- Guidelines for implementing plans and accomplishing change (D: 7 pp 249-256)

REVIEW

The marketing plan (D: 7 pp 242-244)
The marketing plan provides an evaluative framework for identifying corporate problems and alternative solutions. In so doing, it helps to clarify the focus and direction of the marketing effort. The plan itself should be comprehensible and credible and there are many alternative formats which can be used to structure the information it contains. An example framework (D: 7 pp 243-244) uses three headings to focus, analyze and identify objectives for each of the following areas:

- The present position and prognosis
- Marketing objectives
- Marketing strategies
- Competitive reactions
- Marketing programmes
- Tactics and action plans
- Evaluation and control
- Financial forecasts

Conventionally, a written marketing plan constitutes the culmination of a process of information gathering and analysis. However, if it is to be of practical value, it should contain a strategy for implementing it. This should addresses among other key points, organizational changes that might be needed, internal barriers that may require resolution and an estimate of the *real* costs of dealing with change issues.

The planning hierarchy
(D: 4 pp 117-120; A: 6 pp 137-158)
Piercy (D: 4 p 118) illustrates the role of the marketing plan in relation to corporate planning, marketing planning and marketing and sales management. In theory at least, it represents a rational sequence of events - from corporate goals and missions to market audits and planning through to action programmes implemented by marketing, sales and product management teams. Piercy comments that the logic of this sequence is impeccable but that it is unrealistic for practical marketing planning. This is because organizations and the people they employ, rarely operate in such a well-ordered way. Further, MacDonald (1) among others, cite evidence that few companies actually undertake systematic marketing planning, so why bother to study the steps involved? In response, there are at least two good reasons:
- A marketing planning model provides a useful conceptual framework for integrating the issues of marketing information, strategy and programmes. Even if it functions merely.as a checklist, then it has a useful role.
- If the reality is that few companies actually plan their marketing, then a systematic approach to marketing planning presents an opportunity for managing market-led strategic change. In this, the planning process is the tool for 'mould breaking' and culture change on which market-led change depends.

An overview of the planning process
(B: 27 pp 416-430; D: 7 pp 235-245 and 256-264)
Cannon depicts the marketing plan as a linear sequence of events (B: 27 p 417). Piercy provides a more detailed practical perspective on each planning stage and, drawing from these two sources an overview of the planning process typically involves the following steps.

(a) Conducting a marketing audit

The feasibility of the marketing plan depends in part on the accuracy of the information sources it draws upon. If conducted properly, the marketing audit is the most time-consuming stage of the planning process. Piercy advocates separate audits of market, product, pricing, distribution and communications issues using a *focus, analyze* and *objectives* planning framework (D: 7 pp 237-241). He suggests the following headings and focal issues:

- *Market audit* - customer needs and buying factors; products and customers; key products; marketing priorities and critical success factors; market segmentation; company priorities; market sizing and shares; life cycle and competitive position; competitors; marketing environment; market summary; market priorities; critical success factors; marketing objectives.
- *Product audit* - competitive performance, product dimensions, product lines.
- *Pricing audit* - product pricing, market pricing, price trends, value, price levels.
- *Distribution audit* - channels, channel services, channel shares, marketing resources, concentration.
- *Marketing communications audit* - brand/corporate positioning, decision-making units, external influences, media, media performance.

The *market audit* should encompass an analysis of general business trends and market forces, an activity which is sometimes referred to as 'environmental scanning'. This can be defined as: *"The systematic methods used by an organization to monitor and forecast those forces that are external to and not under the direct control of the organization or its industry."* (2).

(b) An analysis of strengths, weaknesses, opportunities and threats (SWOT)

A SWOT analysis provides a useful integrating mechanism for information relating to key issues and events both inside and outside the firm. It is a subjective analytical technique but it is comparatively easy to complete and is easily understandable by users. Piercy believes that the technique can be made to work effectively and that valuable strategic insights are generated if it is used in a disciplined way. He offers the following guidelines for use:

- *Focused SWOTs* - defined carefully to address a particular issue (such as a specific product market, customer segment, product or pricing policy) should be rigorously and continuously enforced so as to avoid meaningless generalizations.
- *Shared visions* - an effective way of using SWOT analysis is to use it as a focal point for group or team planning. In this context it can provide an integrating mechanism for expressing team consensus about important issues.
- *Customer orientation* - the aim here is to confront the differences between what team members think is important and what customers say is important. Applied in this way, the technique will help to reveal the critical success factors, customer needs and the issues affecting customer satisfaction.
- *Structured strategy generation* - an outcome from completing all four cells of the SWOT matrix, it begins with an interpretation and prioritizing of the issues arising. Thereafter, there are four ways of categorizing the strategic options: (a) matching strategies (a focus on matching internal strengths and external opportunities); (b) conversion strategies (responses to perceived weaknesses and threats); (c) creative strategies (new, creative ideas for business development); (d) iteration (how does the SWOT situational analysis fit the broader interpretation of events?) (D: p. 260 Fig. 7.3).

(c) Set objectives

The marketing audit and SWOT analysis provide a foundation upon which marketing objectives can be established. They should clearly set out the purposes or goals that the firm is seeking to achieve through its strategies and tactics. Further, they should be written so that they are consistent, quantifiable and so that outcomes are measurable, actionable and understandable.

Prior to agreeing objectives, it is advisable to test market assumptions against business forecasts. Hospitality/tourism market forecast information can be obtained from analysts (such as Kleinwort Benson) consultants (such as Pannell Kerr Forster Associates and Horwath Consulting) and other sources of informed opinion and by undertaking statistical projections based on past performance.

(d) Establish strategy and tactics

The purpose of strategy is to guide the marketing direction and effort needed to achieve objectives. A strategy statement should therefore possess the same degree of precision and clarity as the individual objectives it embodies. Tactics, defined after the strategy has been set, guide the specific actions required to manage and manoeuvre the available resources. Their role is to define actions to be taken and specific responsibilities for their implementation and in this, they should present a consistent view of the organization to the marketplace.

(e) Agree costs and timings
Detailed schedules of costs and timings should be used to inform decisions about the final allocation of resources to the marketing plan and to refine the proposals for implementing it.

(f) Establish procedures for evaluating the plan
The time and effort involved in drafting and refining a marketing plan suggests that maximum benefit can be derived from a rigorous evaluative procedure. Its purpose is twofold; to provide an indication of success and to enable learning and consolidation to take place. This helps to ensure that refinements can be made to the marketing planning process in succeeding periods.

Summarizing, a well conceived marketing plan will encompass:
- A comprehensive and systematic analysis of external variables and internal priorities.
- Clarity of purpose in defining objectives, strategy and tactics.
- Close co-operation between marketing, operations and other functional areas.
- A clear understanding of the relationships between costs and marketing effort.

Barriers to effective marketing planning
D: 4 pp 117-120; D 6: 247-249)
To derive maximum benefit from the marketing plan and the other planning activities which surround it, a meaningful form of integration must be achieved. Above all, this should result in the creation of a 'total offering' that customers recognize and want to buy. Ultimately, marketing effectiveness is judged by customers and not by the elegance or sophistication of the planning process itself:

"We may start with grandiose ideas about our missions and our competitive positioning, and how we can achieve these through differentiation and advertising strategy, and the like. However, what matters is the reality of what this turns into in the marketplace (i.e. what the customer receives, perceives, and consequently evaluates)."
(D: 4 p 120.)

The key issue here is that 'effectiveness' may be perceived differently internally and by the marketplace. The gap between the two is determined by the difference between intentions and reality:

- *Intended strategy (intent)* - what *we* (the firm) thinks or wants the business to be about in the marketplace.
- *Perceived strategy (reality)* - what the business is *actually* about in the marketplace, as

perceived by the people who run the business, and its customers.

Piercy identifies a number of common problems which impede the effectiveness of marketing planning. These are:

- *Analysis instead of planning* - occurs when planning becomes bogged down with analytical techniques and models which are far removed from the reality they are supposed to represent.
- *Information instead of decision* - can cause planning to disintegrate into a quest for more and better information.
- *Incrementalism* - occurs when the main determinant of a plan is the previous plan or budget.
- *Vested interests rule* - when powerful managers intervene so as to protect budgets and head counts, build empires or achieve other counter-productive goals.
- *Organizational 'mind-set'* - by definition many planning processes are inward-looking and bounded by established codes and conventions.
- *Resistance to marketing change* - may come from other departments or organizational interest groups who feel threatened by the prospects of market-led change.
- *No 'ownership' or commitment* - in the absence of 'champions' determined to make them work, efforts to make plans happen may fail.
- *No resourcing* - there are numerous scenarios, ranging from outright refusal to commit resources to acceptance of the plan but rejection of the accompanying resource request.
- *No implementation* - failure to devise and action a suitable strategy for implementation is a key reason for the failure of marketing plans.
- *Diminishing effort and interest* - if planning is seen as no more than an annual ritual, then efforts and interest may diminish over time.

Guidelines for implementing plans and accomplishing change (D: 7 pp 249-256)
Piercy asserts that the 'real management agenda' for effective planning and market-led change revolves around four issues:

- *Techniques and formalization* - credible plans require a formal planning system supported by appropriate analytical and evaluative techniques.
- *Behavioural issues* - managerial perceptions of the planning process, their motivation to make planning work effectively and their commitment to planning are critical to its success. The key variables here are training for the planning job and ensuring a climate of participation exists throughout the organization.

- *Organizational issues* - the extent to which the organization is supportive of the planning effort is manifest in the example set by managers, the resourcing of planning and recognition of the outcomes of effective planning.
- *Consistency* - in terms of the way in which planning process activities are analyzed and managed.

CONCLUSION

Effective marketing planning requires a balance between the process used and the action taken. This involves formal, systematic procedures for analysis, generation and evaluation (the process) and organizational commitment and participation in the ensuing action. Piercy offers a summary of the key issues that underpin effective marketing planning:

- Make SWOT analysis work;
- Challenge assumptions with marketing intelligence;
- 'Champion' the planning process to make it happen;
- Manage participation; prevent myopic thinking by turning planning upside-down and inside-out;
- Make ownership of ideas and programmes the top priority and work for consistency in the planning approach.

References:

1.   M.MacDonald. *Marketing Plans,* Heinemann, London, 1984.
2.   L.L.Byars. *Strategic Management: Planning and Implementation: Concepts and Cases,* Harper and Row, New York, 1987.

Review exercises:

1.   List the student amenities, facilities and services available at your university/college. Include food service, bar and retail outlets (e.g. book shop, bank and supermarket) leisure and recreational provision but exclude student union clubs and societies. Undertake a SWOT analysis and use Piercy's proforma (D: 7 pp 265-267) to structure a report outlining your findings and recommendations.

2.   Devise and justify appropriate marketing planning frameworks for: (a) a regionally-based chain of bistro style restaurants (average unit size - 40 covers) and (b) a national chain of mid-priced hotels (average unit size of 80 bedrooms).

3.   With reference to the two frameworks defined in RE (2), explain how you would: (a) implement marketing planning and (b) monitor its effectiveness.

EXTENSION

Read: Chapter 27 of *Basic Marketing: Principles and Practice* (B: 27 pp 427-430 Case Study 17). Stirling College of Technology

The case study briefly describes the operational scope and options facing an educational establishment. Although the scenario relates to the 1980s, it illustrates some of the principles of marketing planning.

Extension questions:

Write a report to the Principal outlining:

1.   Your analysis of the college's strengths, weaknesses, opportunities and threats.

2.   Your views on how the marketing effort should be organized, with special reference to the split between central and divisional activities.

Practical exercises:

The following exercises should ideally be undertaken in small groups:

1.   Drawing on your knowledge of a hospitality or tourism sector of your choice, devise a specification for your own business. The business should be a regionally-based, multi-unit operation (between 5-10 units). Use Piercy's worksheet (D: 4 p. 129) to assist in defining your main marketing strategy and operational marketing policies.

2.   Write a marketing plan for your business by working through Piercy's diagnostic worksheet 5 (D: 7 pp 291-293) and by using the questions it contains to think about the most suitable structure and approach. Your plan should address priorities set over a 3 year time period.

3.   Prepare a formal presentation to explain and justify the fit between your business concept as specified in PE (1) its marketing strategy and operational marketing policies and your marketing plan.

8

BUDGETING

INTRODUCTION

The term *marketing budget* refers to the direct and overhead costs associated with the marketing function. However, the budget allocation is seldom as straightforward as this definition implies. Every marketing decision has a resource implication and yet, the planning and allocation of resources to marketing is often neglected in the literature. In fact, it is an issue that commands much of the time and attention of marketing managers because as Piercy points out, the marketing budget is critical to the task of making marketing happen:

"Far from being the province of accountants...marketing budgeting is about something of critical importance - how do we get the resources we need to get our marketing act together and then to go away and do it? Put like this, marketing budgeting is an issue of strategic importance, of considerable relevance to whether we make marketing happen, and one where we also need to get our act together." (D: 8 p. 296.)

This chapter examines the factors which affect the budgeting process for marketing and the extent to which an effective process will support marketing action.

In this chapter:
- Marketing planning and budgeting (D: 8 pp 294-297; C: 6 pp 139-140; A: 7 pp 172-176)
- A conventional view of marketing budgeting (D: 7 pp 249-252 and 8 pp 299-305; A: 17 pp 331-335; B: 23 pp 360-362)
- What really determines marketing budgets? (D: 8 pp 305-307; B pp 365-366)
- Analyzing the budgeting process (D: 8 pp 307-317; B: 23 pp 366-367)
- Functional analysis and marketing budgets

REVIEW

Marketing planning and budgeting (D: 8 pp 294-297; C: 6 pp 139-140; A: 7 pp 172-176)
There is an indisputable link between the relative success of a marketing action plan and the readiness of the organization to allocate resources to its implementation. The most commonly re-occurring problems relating to the allocation of resources to marketing include:

- the 'hassle factor' - the investment of valuable time and effort in administrative procedures, form-filling and committees;
- conflict over marketing expenditure with accountants and general management.
- a perceived (or actual) lack of control relating to marketing expenditure.
- a conflict between pro-active, innovative marketing plans and more reactive parts of the organization.

Unfortunately it is often difficult to prove the link between expenditure and marketing effectiveness and this compounds the problem of justifying the allocation of resources to marketing. There are also very real problems in defining the scope of the marketing budget. For instance, advertising costs for a hotel restaurant may not be allocated to that department but shown under the general heading of 'advertising' for the entire operation. Further, the payroll costs of the sales department are relatively easy to identify as marketing expenditure but the sales role of a hotel receptionist is unlikely to be separated from the front office payroll.

The items classified as marketing expenditure vary from company to company and, as there is no universal rule, industry sector comparisons are difficult. In some circumstances the marketing budget may include items over which the marketing department has little jurisdiction. For instance, in some hotel companies, agent's commission and room discounts are set by the finance department and charged to the marketing department. These costs represent a substantial sum and plans submitted by the marketing department to discount heavily in the short stay business market for example, may be rejected because of the commitments made by other departments.

Given the difficulties outlined so far, the marketing budget is more easily defined in relation to the items of expenditure and other resources which are required to implement the marketing plan. Resources will include people, expertise, computer technology and training, among others.

A conventional view of marketing budgeting
(D: 7 pp 249-252 and 8 pp 299-305; A: 17 pp 331-335; B: 23 pp 360-362)
There are three dimensions to the process of marketing budgeting; analytical, behavioural and organizational. Further, the tasks involved are either (a) *prescriptive* or (b) *descriptive* in nature.

(a) Prescriptive approaches

Prescriptive approaches comprise techniques that can be used to evaluate budget requirements. They include:

- *Economic analysis* - based on the economic principle of marginality. This view proposes that spending on marketing should continue until the marginal income from the marginal unit of expenditure is equal to its cost - at this point income exceeds expenditure. The practicality of measuring this in a commercial setting is limited.

- *Management science models* - provide a range of mathematically-based ways of determining the optimum marketing and advertising spend. Although sophisticated, they do have limitations in that they cannot replicate every facet of the marketplace.

- *Corporate budgeting approaches* - such as programmed, output and 'objective and task' methods. The objective and task method is the most commonly used and it works by translating corporate objectives into measurable outputs, such as growth in product sales. It then proposes that specific, costed, marketing action can be taken. The main problem relates to the way in which corporate objectives are interpreted, especially if they have not been quantified in a measurable way.

- *Judgmental budgeting models* - set guidelines for the marketing budget such as 'percentage-of-sales'. The danger of this approach is that budgeting becomes too rigid with little room for contingencies. The same problem can arise from over-dependence on a comparative budgeting approach, which may mean that expenditure levels are set in accordance with competitor spending levels.

- *Sequential models* - utilize a combination of budgeting approaches to construct the budget. Potentially, the problem here is that experience, judgement and intuition, in themselves valuable assets, play a secondary role. Further, there is a risk that the wider organizational view is underestimated if efforts to plan objectively and rationally fail to take account of subjective opinion and debate within the organization.

(b) Descriptive approaches

Examine how budgeting actually happens in organizations, they include:

- *Precedents* - usually work on the principle that the previous year's marketing budget provides a basis for negotiating the current year's budget. Alternatives like building the budget from a 'zero base' each year are complex and time-consuming to implement.

- *Incrementalism* - budgets tend to remain relatively constant from year-to-year, but much management time and attention is taken-up with discussing and agreeing budget variations for the purposes of achieving specific marketing objectives.

- *Calculation models* - in addition to other approaches, managers may have to base budget decisions on what is affordable. In so doing, it may be necessary to justify budget figures by referring to sector-specific expenditure figures published in advertising yearbooks.

- *Experiential* - experience and intuition are important aspects of the budget-setting process. Observing marketing outcomes from particular forms of expenditure and competitive activity can provide clues for future action.

- *Negotiation* - the reality of securing budget approval is that some form of negotiation and/or bargaining is inevitable in most organizations. Negotiating effectiveness is greatly enhanced by budget-setting activities based on robust calculations and projections.

What really determines marketing budgets?
(D: 8 pp 305-307; B pp 365-366)

Piercy suggests that marketing budgets are influenced by all or at least, some of the following factors:

- *Power* - of the marketing department relative to other parts of the organization, in terms of organizational structures, participation in important decisions and status.

- *Strategic contingencies* - put simply, this issue can be expressed in the form of a question. How critical to its success in attracting and retaining specific groups of customers is a particular programme of marketing action?

- *Process control* - relates to the rules and agenda-setting for the marketing budgeting process. Who participates in the budget discussions and decision-making and how are the criteria for budget decisions defined and applied?

It is often the case that these activities are led, or strongly influenced by, accountants or general managers with specific operational experience such as food and beverage management.

- *Political influence* - who influences the executive decision-making process? The personalities of the people involved constitute an important factor in the internal debate about how resources are allocated.

- *Bargaining and advocacy* - effective negotiating skills and an ability to build and promote the case for marketing expenditure are key ingredients in the bid for a share of organizational resources.

- *Corporate culture* - the acceptability of resource bids for marketing is partially determined by the culture and business orientation of the company. For example, some hotel companies still retain a product-led focus and may resist market-led change initiatives.

Analyzing the budgeting process
(D: 8 pp 307-317; B: 23 pp 366-367)
To ensure that the projected costs of marketing action are logically and systematically evaluated, procedures for setting the marketing budget should consider the following issues:

- The extent to which the procedures for marketing planning and budgeting are connected. Budgeting should be an integral part of the marketing planning process. Efforts to explain the resource implications of marketing action are more straightforward when they relate to specific marketing objectives.

- The extent to which marketing and other appropriate personnel have been able to contribute to and/or assist in verifying the accuracy of costs and the proposed allocation of marketing expenditure.

- The overall acceptability of marketing planning and budgeting proposals to the organization. Are the proposed actions and costs related to the organization's mission, direction and corporate objectives? All too often the maintenance of *status quo* is an overriding consideration. If so, market-led change will require careful planning and costing so as to avoid direct conflict.

Piercy offers a diagnostic test which can be used to assess the effectiveness of the budgeting process (D: 8 pp 314-317). The diagnostic covers four areas: (a) budget-setting techniques in marketing; (b) the control of marketing budgeting; (c) the marketing budgeting process; (d) key personnel and their involvement. A checklist of statements is provided to help users to more fully explore the mechanics of their own organization's marketing budgeting system and to consider how it may relate to other corporate issues such as market orientation and strategic direction.

Functional analysis and marketing budgets
Marketing budgeting is a relative process in that the level of functional expenditure is ultimately determined by what the organization can afford, by prevailing market forces and the activities of its principal competitors (1). In the food industry, the manufacture of convenience food snacks such as crisps is based on technology which is well known and developed and widely available. In these circumstances, the primary issue in the battle to secure market share relates to product differentiation and ultimately, marketing strength. Most food snacks are not essential food items and indeed there is a body of opinion that is highly critical of the role of convenience food snacks in the diet. Therefore, concentrated marketing is important to counter this view and to maintain the profile of the brand in a highly competitive marketplace.

Arguably, most hospitality and tourism organizations *can* differentiate and position their products without recourse to high levels of marketing expenditure. This is partly because services are inherently more complex and so the customer must become more actively involved in choosing between competing products. If the issue of product differentiation can be successfully addressed, resource allocation for functional areas like marketing and operations can be determined by a balanced approach to assessing market and organizational needs and priorities.

CONCLUSION

Budgeting for marketing action should be regarded as an integral part of the marketing planning process so that the allocation of resources is specifically related to agreed objectives. It is however, a contentious and often politically charged activity given the finite resources that organizations have at their disposal.

Many of the difficulties encountered when negotiating marketing budgets within organizations can be overcome, but among other considerations, it requires a rational justification for changes from prior budget levels, based on identified market needs and agreed objectives.

Piercy provides a helpful summary perspective:

"...budgeting for marketing is frequently a highly problematic area for executives due to the organizational realities of getting marketing resourced...the important point is that we should see marketing budgeting as a process, and as a process that is inseparable from the marketing planning process. The underlying truth is that all too often marketing seems to happen in spite of the attitude of companies towards budgets and head-counts. If we are serious about market-led strategic change, then we cannot escape the conclusion that it comes with a price-tag." (D8 pp 312-313.)

Reference:

1. P.McNamee. *Management Accounting - Strategic Planning and Marketing,* Heinemann, London, pp 125-143, 1988.

Review questions:

1. Explain why financial management policies and accounting departments in hospitality /tourism organizations may have undue influence over the marketing budgeting process.

2. Evaluate the use of *prescriptive* approaches to marketing budget-setting in a medium to large hotel company.

3. Anticipate the stages and timing in marketing budget setting for a large, private city centre leisure facility. Discuss the organizational issues that may have to be addressed before the budget is finalized.

EXTENSION

Read: Chapter 20 of *Essentials of Marketing* (C: 20 pp 462-489) *(Case study with specimen answer: Apex Leisure Ltd.).*

This case study describes the situation of Apex Leisure Ltd. The company is facing a number of problems that threaten the long term future of the venture.

The new club director has proposed an approach to reverse the current adverse trading situation and there is also the possibility of the acquisition of another property for commercial use.

Extension questions:

You are required to complete a marketing audit and SWOT analysis of the company and draft an outline marketing plan for the operation. Then answer the following questions:

1. Evaluate the use of descriptive approaches to budget-setting using examples from the case.

2. What are the organizational implications of the opportunities that you have identified?

3. Evaluate the main demands on resources from the functional departments described.

Practical exercises:

You have been appointed as marketing manager directly answerable to the club director. You have been asked to prepare the draft of a marketing budget for a meeting in two days time. The club director is anxious to receive a marketer's view of what is possible and has asked you to address the following issues without reference to the club accountant:

1. From the information given in the case, draft an approximate income and expenditure statement for the next four years of operation. Your statement should be categorized so as to include approximate income contributed by the different income generating departments and areas of the club.

2. Identify and comment on the main marketing objectives, tasks and priorities to be set over a four year period and include *approximate* budget costings. You may have to refer to industry statistics and marketing year books in your library to complete this exercise.

3. Prepare a position statement anticipating the objections which may be raised by senior management and department heads and explain how you will counter their objections.

9
SEGMENTATION

INTRODUCTION

"The marketer should stop thinking of his customers as part of some massively homogeneous market. He must start thinking of them as numerous small islands of distinctiveness, each of which requires its own unique strategies in product policy, in promotional strategy, in pricing, in distribution methods, and in direct selling techniques."
T. Levitt, *Marketing for Business Growth*, McGraw-Hill, New York, 1974, p. 69.

While market diversification was a generic strategy for the 1980s, market segmentation has become a predominant theme of the 1990s. Many companies previously developing products for diverse markets, have found the resource implications unsustainable as customer demand has dwindled. This has led to greater emphasis on defining the characteristics of accessible and financially viable customer groups in order to position an existing product portfolio and rationalize production and marketing costs in the process. The nature of hospitality and tourism services facilitate both product and market differentiation with enhanced opportunities for cost control and productivity gains. This chapter seeks to explore the segmentation methods available for this purpose.

In this chapter:
- Market segmentation and target marketing (C: 7 pp 157-158; B: 7 pp 131-134; A: 5 pp 115-120)
- Market segmentation - evaluative criteria (A: 5 pp 117-133; B: 7 pp 133-138)
- Bases for segmenting consumer markets (C: 7 pp 160-176; A: 5 pp 120-131; B: 7 pp 133-137; B: 12 pp 208-219)

REVIEW

Market segmentation and target marketing
(C: 7 pp 157-158; B: 7 pp 131-134; A: 5 pp 115-120)
The terms 'target marketing' and 'market segmentation' are often used interchangeably but there is a slight difference of emphasis. The concept of target marketing is a refinement of the basic philosophy of marketing. It is an attempt by companies to relate the characteristics or attributes of the goods and services they provide more closely to customer requirements.

Market segmentation is a part of the overall process of target marketing. Thus Kotler (1) states that the process of target marketing has three distinct stages:

- *Market segmentation.* The overall market is divided into distinct groups of buyers who are likely to respond favourably to different product/service offerings and market mixes. Examples of discrete market segments include short stay business travellers and families with young children.

- *Market targeting.* The process whereby one or more of the market segments previously identified are evaluated and selected. For instance short stay business travellers (midweek) and families with young children at weekends.

- *Product positioning.* Competition exists for identified market segments in 'niche' positions. Product positioning is the process whereby the product or service and all the other marketing mix elements are designed to fit a given place within a particular segment. The position is often defined by communications such as advertising rather than actual product differences.

Market segmentation - evaluative criteria
(A: 5 pp 117-133; B: 7 pp 133-138)
The process of market segmentation should be contained by specified evaluative criteria. This is because there is a danger that unrestrained segmentation can lead to an unsustainable range of product modifications and produce similar disbenefits to market diversification. Criteria for assessing potential segments include:

- *Profitable size.* The relative profit potential in a segment is directly related to the competitive strength and cost effectiveness of the company. Even a small market may be profitable if the company has a competitive edge.

- *Accessibility.* A segment must be accessible through advertising, other promotional media, and distributive networks.

- *Self containment.* A new product launch or re-positioning for a specific market segment should not undermine demand for existing products /services in the company's range.

- *Marketing mix response.* The market segment should be responsive to marketing and promotional effort.

Bases for segmenting consumer markets
(C: 7 pp 160-176; A: 5 pp 120-131; B: 7 pp 133-137;
B: 12 pp 208-219)

(a) Demographic
Demographic segmentation is one of the most
straightforward and meaningful bases for segmenting
markets. The principal demographic categories are
age, family size and life cycle, and social status and
income.

Age. For many products buyer behaviour is closely
related to age category. The range of this category
will vary depending upon the product or service - a
discotheque will appeal to an 18-30 age range,
whereas visiting historic properties is likely to be
more popular with a 25-45 age range. Age is
routinely used as a segmentation variable to
characterize the behaviour of markets. A more
meaningful analysis of buyer behaviour can
sometimes be obtained by combining age and gender
variables.

Family size and life cycle. Many consumption
patterns are taught and developed within the family
unit and life cycle. Family life cycle, combined with
income and occupation is used by Research Services
(2) to delineate different consumer groups. First,
consumers are sub-divided into one of four life cycle
groups: *(a) dependent adults* (single adults); *(b) pre-
family* (adults married without children); *(c) family*
(one or more children); *(d) late* (adults whose
children have left home). The four life cycle groups
are then further sub-divided by a combination of
occupation and/or income into one of twelve major
groupings, branded by Research Services as
'SAGACITY'. Evidence suggests that SAGACITY is
a powerful discriminator between consumer groups
for a wide range of products and services.

Social class/income. The current convention in the
UK is to use a mix of social class and income
variables. Social classification is based on the
occupation of the head of household. Socio-
economic classifications used in the UK are those
established by the National Readership Survey, as
follows:

A   higher managerial, administrative or
    professional;
B   intermediate managerial, administrative and
    professional;
C1 supervisory, clerical, junior administrative or
    professional;
C2 skilled manual workers;
D   semi and unskilled manual workers;
E   state pensioners, widows, lowest grade workers.

Despite criticisms relating to the inadequacies of this
classification (such as the generalized assumptions it
makes) it is a widely used method. However, it
should be noted that there are discrepancies within
and between the categories because occupation and
income variables are not consistently interrelated.

(b) Geo-demographic
This approach to segmentation combines a number
of variables such as where a customer lives, with
home ownership and size of family. They are
particularly relevant to the location and development
of hospitality/tourism operations such as pubs,
restaurants and leisure facilities. One approach to
geo-demographic segmentation using geographic,
cultural, socio-economic and other factors is 'A
Classification of Residential Neighbourhoods' or
ACORN. The ACORN system is a method of
mapping geographically the concentrations of
particular types of people. The assumption is that the
demographic/socio-economic characteristics of
people can be correlated to the housing
characteristics of a particular area.

The ACORN classifications are derived using a
multi-variable statistical treatment of census
population data and are divided into ACORN groups
and sub-divided into ACORN types. There are
eleven ACORN groups:

A   agricultural areas;
B   modern family housing, higher incomes;
C   older housing of intermediate status;
D   poor-quality older terraced housing;
E   better-off council estates;
F   less well-off council estates;
G   poorest council estates;
H   multi-racial areas;
I   high-status non-family areas;
J   affluent suburban housing;
K   better-off retirement areas.

The main groups have further sub-divisions known
as ACORN types. For example, group B has five
sub-categories:

B3 cheap modern private housing;
B4 recent private housing, young families;
B5 modern private housing, older children;
B6 new detached houses, young families;
B7 military bases.

(c) Benefit and behavioural segmentation
Benefit segmentation uses *causal* rather than
descriptive variables to group consumers. Different
people buy the same or similar products for different
reasons.

For instance, some people will visit a restaurant because it has a reputation for good food or drink and therefore seek a gastronomic experience, others may visit the same restaurant to derive social benefits or status. Haley (3) first introduced this approach which is based on the assumption that consumers can be grouped according to the principal benefit sought from a product or service.

Behavioural segmentation focuses on the consumption rates for a product or service as a means of segmenting markets. For instance, users of a leisure centre may be classified as: frequent users (daily visits); less frequent users (at least once a week); users (occasional visits) or non-users. If a company can identify the characteristics of its frequent users (they may live in a certain area and have other common features such as income) it can target concentrate some of its marketing effort on a programme which aims to increase the number of frequent users and the overall size of this segment.

Loyalty status. A market can also be segmented according to the relative degree of loyalty exhibited by customers to a given product or service. Kotler (1) identifies four groups for this purpose each characterized by different levels of consumer loyalty. Kotler's loyalty status approach is illustrated by the following example.

A brewery identifies four pubs in a given postal code area, referred to here as pub A, pub B, pub C and pub D. The next step is to classify the local pub user population and using Kotler's classification, the pub loyalty patterns are as follows:

- *Hard core loyals* - these are customers with undivided loyalty to one particular pub. Their purchase pattern for six visits is AAAAAA.

- *Soft core loyals* - are represented by customers with divided loyalty between two or more pubs. The purchase pattern for six visits is AABBBA.

- *Shifting loyalties* - customers who routinely 'brand switch'. The purchase pattern for six visits is ACBAAC.

- *Switchers* - made-up of customers who demonstrate no purchase pattern loyalty to a particular pub. In this instance, the purchase pattern for six visits is ACDBAD.

Depending upon the nature of the product the competitive situation and the resources available, it is possible to influence loyalty patterns so as to increase the number of hard and soft core loyal users.

(d) Psychographic and life style segmentation
Some of the previously mentioned segmentation methods such as demographics and social classification may be too narrow to portray the wide variations in behaviour and outlook of a target population. Life style and psychographic segmentation seek to remedy this situation.

Both methods attempt to cluster consumers into groups based on common interests and attitudes which determine the way they spend their time and money. Thus, the AB socio-economic group could be sub-divided into life style 'leisure groups' which may include:

- '*Young aspiring sophisticate*' - generally well educated and gregarious, enjoys clubs and societies, interested in new leisure ideas.

- '*Young fogey*' - generally conservative, well educated, enjoys traditional pursuits, country sports, resists new ideas.

Life style segmentation can be used to classify specific markets for products groups such as food and drink products and chain restaurant operations. The research needed to develop specific life style groups can be expensive and difficult to interpret but it can also be very revealing. If customer attitudes, interests and opinions can be linked to purchase loyalty patterns for example, it becomes easier to devise and target appropriate marketing programmes.

(e) Business-to-business
A substantial proportion of the overall demand for hospitality and tourism services comes from other businesses and organizations. For example, demand for conferences, seminars, incentive travel packages and air crew services among others, is generated by businesses (industrial markets) rather than consumer markets. The concept of segmentation can therefore be applied, although the bases used are likely to be different (4). Some of the most frequently used variables for segmenting industrial markets are: type of industry; type of organization; size of firm and geographical region.

CONCLUSION

Slow and in most cases static growth in mature markets, volatile consumer demand and more, better organized competition means that companies are finding it increasingly difficult and expensive to practice mass marketing techniques. Crawford-Welch summarizes the key role that market segmentation now plays in product development, competitive positioning and in justifying a wide array of marketing decisions:

"Segmentation in the international hospitality industry will continue to be a force to be reckoned with for several reasons. First, conventional wisdom in the field of financial management suggests that firms should keep a portfolio of businesses to balance their earnings stream. In theory, the portfolio is designed so that the return to the shareholder will be stable over the life of the firm. Thus, individual businesses are expected to compliment each other such that when one business is experiencing a downturn the other businesses will be up. It is in response to this type of thinking that hospitality firms began to develop multiple brands. Second, segmentation offers hospitality firms the opportunity to grow in a saturated marketplace. Third it is often cheaper and financially wiser to build new concepts than to renovate existing hotel room inventory. In the USA for example, it is estimated that over 50 per cent of today's inventory in the lodging industry is old and tired." (F: 11 p. 171.)

Hospitality, tourism and other service organizations are in the enviable position of dealing directly with the customer and so they are well-placed to analyze customer profiles and buyer behaviour patterns. Further, advances in computer technology and its availability to firms of all sizes facilitate this form of analysis and support sophisticated segmentation research. This in turn, will help to improve the effectiveness of target marketing as a means of focusing scarce resources more precisely.

References:

1. P.Kotler, *Marketing Management, Analysis and Control.* 7th ed. Prentice Hall, NY, 1991.
2. Research Services Ltd., *SAGACITY: A Special Analysis of JICNAR'S* NRS 1980 *Data.* London, 1981.
3. R.I.Haley, 'Benefit Segmentation: A Decision Oriented Tool', *Journal of Marketing,* July, 1968, pp 30-35.
4. F.E.Webster and Y. Wind, *Organizational Buying Behaviour.* Prentice Hall, NY, 1989.

Review questions:

1. Using behavioural and benefit variables, devise a suitable segmentation strategy for a city centre, fast food operation with a high proportion of take-away sales.

2. How would you evaluate the commercial viability of the segmentation criteria identified in (1) above?

3. Explain life style segmentation and its use in defining hospitality/tourism markets.

EXTENSION

Read: Chapter 20 of *Essentials of Marketing* (C: 20 pp 462-489) *(Case study with specimen answer: Apex Leisure Ltd.).*

This case study describes the situation of Apex Leisure Ltd. The company is facing a number of problems that threaten the long term future of the venture.

The new club director has proposed an approach to reverse the current adverse trading situation and there is also the possibility of the acquisition of another property for commercial use.

Extension questions:

You are required to complete a marketing audit and SWOT analysis of the company and draft an outline marketing plan for the operation. Then answer the following questions:

1. Identify appropriate market segments for Crispins and Acotts Manor using the full range of segmentation variables.

2. Explain the implications for developing a marketing strategy based on the variables identified in (1) above.

3. Outline a communication strategy for the two operations, including a media plan based on the segmentation variables identified in (1) above.

Practical exercises:

1. Select *two* hospitality/tourism organizations and using their company reports, identify the principal demographic/benefit segmentation variables for their products and services.

2. Devise and justify appropriate consumer life style groups for the range of goods and services offered by the two companies and comment on the marketing implications of your proposal.

3. Identify the respective business and organizational markets for the two companies, explain how you would segment them and comment on the implications for product /service development.

10
PRODUCT, PRICING AND DISTRIBUTION

INTRODUCTION

"The essence of managing the marketing mix lies in providing each group of customers or segment of the market with a mix of product, price, place [distribution] and promotion which most suits their needs. The product manager is in many ways turning the product or brand into a market in its own right." (B: 17 p. 280).

The effectiveness of the marketing mix depends on the fit between manageable resources (mix elements) and the needs of specific customer groups. The aim of this chapter is to examine the respective contributions made by three of the mix elements - the product and its pricing and distribution.

In this chapter:
- The product (A: 8; 9 and 10 pp 184-232; B: 17 and 18 pp 279-285 and 286-300; C: 8 pp 179-211)
- The price (A: 11 and 12 pp 234-274; B: 17 and 20 pp 279-285 and 318-329; C: 9 pp 212-227)
- The distribution (A: 13 and 14 pp 276-290 and 297; B: 17; 21 and 22 pp 279-285; 330-337 and 338-347; C: 10 pp 228-255)

REVIEW

The product (A: 8; 9 and 10 pp 184-232; B: 17 and 18 pp 279-285 and 286-300; C: 8 pp 179-211)

"The product is the most important element of the marketing mix, since it holds together promotion, distribution and pricing policies." (B: 18 p. 286).

A product has different definitions according to the background of the person who is defining it. A technician or operative can provide a technical specification of the product, while a marketer is more likely to define a product in relation to its function and customer benefits. The American Marketing Association define a product as anything that can be offered to a market for attention, acquisition or consumption, including physical objects, services, personalities, organizations and desires.

Products can be seen has having two dimensions: *features* and *benefits*. Benefits have to do with the satisfaction the product delivers to the customer, while features are the physical characteristics designed into a product, so that it can deliver satisfaction to the customer. In fact, the real nature of the product lies in the customer's perception of it.

Sometimes the product which the marketer wants to create and deliver may be quite different from that received by the customer. It is important therefore to distinguish between the core, tangible and augmented components of a product (1).
- The *core product* is the fundamental benefit which the customer receives.
- The *tangible product* is the way the fundamental benefit is translated physically.
- The *augmented product* is the complete product offering.

The *product mix* represents the complete range of products offered by a marketer. It is necessary here to draw some distinctions between product class and product line, and between product type, brand and item:
- A *product class* is a group of products which deliver the same core benefits.
- A *product line* is a major sub-division of a product class in which the products are closely related.
- A *product type* is a sub-division of a product line, closely related by form.
- A *brand* is symbolized by a word or words and/or graphic, used to identify the product(s) of a specific producer. In many cases, it is possible to describe a brand by referring to the characteristics or 'personality' with which the product is imbued. Hotel brands like Forte Crest offer a distinctive set of services, amenities and facilities that conform to a standard operational blueprint.
- An *item* is a specific unit offered to the market - e.g. every outlet of a restaurant chain can be viewed as a product unit.

If it is to be successful, three product mix variables will need to be manipulated and controlled. These are: *product width* (the number of different lines), *product depth* (the number of items in each line) and *product consistency* (adherence to product specifications for manufacture, supply and service).

The importance of product branding in the marketplace is often reflected in the organizational structure of marketing departments. Here, product or brand management positions provide focal points for integrating and co-ordinating production and marketing effort.

If an organization's marketing effort is brand-based, it is generally to try to ensure that customers perceive a difference in the nature of the brand and its rival offerings. A brand achieves distinctiveness when it is *differentiated* in the mind of the customer. A more complete definition incorporates this perspective by describing a brand as:

"...a name, term, symbol, design or combination of these which is intended to identify the goods or services of one seller or group of sellers and to differentiate them from those of other sellers." (B: 18 p. 289).

New products play an important role in reinforcing competitive strength and positioning in the marketplace. The way in which a new product is launched and presented to potential buyers therefore requires careful consideration. For example, a re-launched product can appear new if different benefits are promoted, whether or not these are tangible or intangible, without radically altering its appearance or performance. What really matters is that the customer perceives the product offered as being different from the existing offering.

There are several ways of categorizing new products (C: 8 p. 185):
- *Innovative products.* These are products that are truly new to the customer. They provide totally different alternatives to existing products which serve existing markets.
- *Replacement products.* These are replacements for existing products and although not wholly innovative, they can provide a significant form of differentiation from those that are currently on offer.
- *Imitative products.* This category covers products that are new to a company, but are already well established in the marketplace. They follow on from the replacements and innovations, developed initially by individual firms. Imitative products are sometimes described as 'me-too' products because they imply a certain lack of novelty or imagination on the behalf of the firm launching them.

The *Product life cycle (PLC)* is an important concept within the overall product policy. It assumes that once the product or service has reached the market, it will be subject to a 'life cycle' and will eventually fade from the market. This concept is used for examining product growth and development, but it is worth mentioning that PLC theory doesn't necessarily apply in all cases or in a predictable and consistent way. There are four stages in the pattern of demand during the product's life cycle: *introduction, growth, maturity,* and *decline.*

Each stage can exhibit different characteristics according to the sales behaviour of items, brands, types, lines, or classes of products. The firm can try to exploit the life cycle by looking for new product developments, innovations or new markets to extend the life cycle.

- *Introduction stage.* This stage is characterized by conditions that relate to those of a new product launch, namely a high product failure rate, relatively little competition, limited distribution, frequent product modification, and company losses (due to costs not yet recouped). Promotion is directed at creating product awareness.
- *Growth stage.* This stage is characterized by more competitors, rising sales, profitable returns, and company or product acquisitions by larger companies. Promotion emphasis on the brand or trade name, and the promotional budget, relative to sales, should allow room for a profit return.
- *Maturity stage.* This is the longest stage of the life cycle. Sales continue to increase, but at a reduced rate, while prices and profits begin to fall. Promotional strategy is directed at reinforcement of the message in order to encourage re-buys.
- *Decline stage.* A combination of factors (market dynamics and competition, new product innovations and changes in customer preferences), can contribute to a decline in sales and signify that the product has entered the decline stage. This is further characterized by falling sales for the entire industry sector (in mature markets), price-cutting, and a decision by some producers to withdraw products or even to withdraw from the marketplace. The key strategic decision is whether to leave the market and concentrate resources on new markets, or try to rejuvenate sales.

The price (A: 11 and 12 pp 234-274; B: 17 and 20 pp 279-285 and 318-329; C: 9 pp 212-227)

"...the economics of supply and demand require that hotels use segmented prices to maximize revenues and attempt to cover the property's large fixed investment. Most hotels now use what can best be described as a 'haggling' approach to attempt to segment customers." (2).

Price is the mechanism of exchange between the firm and its customers. More specifically, it is the amount for which the product, service and idea is exchanged or offered for sale, regardless of its worth or value to potential purchasers.

Pricing policy has to fulfil a number of important roles. These include:

- fusing together the various elements of company activity necessary to meet customer requirements;
- ensuring that the many sources of cost incurred in production, service and delivery are recovered;
- generating residual profits in keeping with company objectives.

Pricing is a strategic issue because policy adjustments ultimately affect profit and loss-making situations. It is therefore important to ensure that pricing policy decisions are closely linked to a wider framework of decision-making including:

- The overall context set by marketing objectives and strategy.
- Adjustments made to the other elements of the marketing mix and the overall coherence and consistency of the mix.
- The need to ensure that cost inputs are not over emphasized in pricing decisions.
- The need to ensure that pricing does not become the overriding factor in thinking and planning competitive strategy and tactics.
- Systematic procedures for reviewing the relationships between cost and profit margins, administered jointly by the accounting and marketing departments.

The policy framework for pricing decisions should also take account of the processes and procedures governing: (a) pricing and company objectives; (b) the role of pricing in strategy formulation and implementation; (c) methods for determining specific pricing levels; (d) the administration of price changes; and (e) credits and discounts.

The distribution (A: 13 and 14 pp 276-290 and 297; B: 17; 21 and 22 pp 279-285; 330-337 and 338-347; C: 10 pp 228-255)
Distribution makes the product physically available. through *distribution channels* or by *physical distribution*. Accordingly, distribution decisions relate to (a) overall channel strategy; (b) the role of intermediaries in distribution; (c) outlets; (d) warehouse and production locations; (e) service levels; (f) systems and documentation for logistics and distribution; (g) geographical coverage; (h) stock levels, freight costs and insurance.

The channel management role is primarily concerned with ensuring that the product is accessible to the customer. Channels are the networks of intermediaries linking or capable of linking the producer and the product to the market.

For example, UK hotel companies use the major multiple retail travel agency chains to sell UK leisure breaks. This distribution channel ensures that the short break product represented by a brochure, is highly visible and accessible to high street shoppers.

Distribution channel decisions are generally medium to long term arrangements as it is difficult and costly to make frequent adjustments to the channel strategy. This is because agreements with intermediaries are usually covered by fixed term contracts. Further, alterations to the channel network may involve costly changes to information systems and high marketing costs to ensure that end users are fully informed of new distribution arrangements.

From a marketing perspective, the construction or modification of a distribution channel presents four options:

- *Intensive distribution*. This involves seeking every possible outlet for the firm's product.
- *Selective distribution*. Here the producer limits distribution to several intermediaries. There are several possible reasons for adopting this approach, but it is most likely to occur if the selected distributor(s) has many, geographically dispersed outlets, (in the case of national or regional distribution) or if distribution in one or several regions is the main requirement.
- *Exclusive distribution*. The producer selects the intermediary very carefully in order to maximize the synergistic potential of the relationship. This approach is well suited to the retail of luxury products.
- *Vertical integration*. If sales volume is directly related to the number of distribution outlets, as it is for beer sales for instance, ownership or control of the means of distribution is beneficial. In this example the brewer (the producer) will actively seek to expand the number and type of outlets by acquiring or building pubs. Additionally, agreements with other brewers and with retailers can be used to extend the scope of distribution.

Physical distribution is concerned with the logistical relationships between production, warehousing, inventory levels, outlet location, and transportation. The degree of interconnectivity between these aspects of physical distribution calls for effective co-ordination and integration. If the functions of production, sales and distribution are not closely aligned, errors and delays will occur in end-user support and supply. So, effective communications and efficient systems are vitally important to the link between the organization and its customers.

The efficiency of physical distribution can be monitored by assessing its internal efficiency and external customer support:

- *Internal efficiencies* - can be achieved by ensuring that all aspects of the physical distribution system operate harmoniously and with appropriate levels of operational and sales liaison.
- *External services* - can be assessed by monitoring the organization's ability to ensure that its products and services are available at the time, in the place, and in the condition required by its customers.

CONCLUSION

The product with its features and benefits has to satisfy the needs and wants of customers. In terms of the marketing mix, it has core, tangible and augmented components which can be manipulated in relation to its market positioning, stage in the life cycle, pricing and distribution. Pricing decisions ultimately help to determine the success or failure of a product in the marketplace. Distribution is concerned with ensuring that the right product reaches the right customer, or in the case of a hotel or restaurant operation, that the outlet where production and consumption takes place, is geared to the needs of target customers. As competition increases, the importance of channel management and physical distribution grows proportionately as a successful distribution policy will ensure that the product is visible and accessible in the marketplace.

References:

1.   P.Kotler. *Marketing Management: Analysis, Planning and Control*. 5th Ed., Prentice-Hall, Englewood Cliffs, NY, 1984, pp. 463-4.

2.   R.D.Hanks, R.G.Cross, and R.P.Noland. 'Discounting in the Hotel Industry: A New Approach.' *The Cornell Hotel and Restaurant Administration Quarterly*, February, 1992.

Review questions:

1.   What are the differences between the product mix, product class and product line? Use hospitality/tourism examples to illustrate your answer.

2.   Why are pricing decisions strategic? Support your answer by explaining the impact of price changes relating to a product/service of your choice.

3.   Evaluate the contribution of channel management and/or physical distribution to the success of a product/service of your choice.

EXTENSION

Read: 'Discounting in the Hotel Industry: A New Approach.' by R.D.Hanks, R.G.Cross, and R.P.Noland. *The Cornell Hotel and Restaurant Administration Quarterly*, February, 1992.

This article addresses the issue of price discounting and debates whether restrictive pricing options are helpful or not to hotel operators and customers. The authors conclude by outlining a rational approach to price segmentation.

Note: If this article is not available in your library, select an alternative article to use in conjunction with the questions below.

Extension questions:

1.   Select a hospitality operation and define its core product. Differentiate between the core and tangible components and list the ways in which the product is, or could be augmented.

2.   Explain the issues which influence: (a) product-line pricing and (b) pricing to take account of different stages in the product life cycle. Use illustrations to support your views.

3.   Which channel intermediaries might contribute to the marketing of (a) self catering apartments; (b) city break holidays; (c) a theme park?

Practical exercises:

1.   Select three hospitality/tourism products each at different stages of the life cycle and analyze the respective price and distribution strategies appropriate to their needs.

2.   Using one of the products identified in (1) above, demonstrate how the price element is related to, and consistent with the other elements of the marketing mix.

3.   A large tour operator is about to launch a new product for a river cruises market. Explain how you would establish suitable channel intermediaries for the distribution of this product.

11
ADVERTISING, PUBLIC RELATIONS AND PROMOTION

INTRODUCTION

"Advertising and sales promotion are the most obvious aspects of the marketing effort. To many people, they are synonymous with marketing itself. Media advertising stares down from posters, enters the home through television, radio and newspapers and is in the workplace through the industrial, trade and technical press." (B: 23 p. 348).

Advertising, public relations and sales promotion are the means by which organizations communicate with their customers. The purpose is to influence perceptions, attitudes and behaviour, either to increase sales or to improve the image of the organization. In this context, the aim of the chapter is to examine the factors influencing the successful design and implementation of this activity.

In this chapter:
- Advertising (A: 16 and 17 pp 315-355; B: 23 pp 348-371; C: 11 pp 273-289)
- Public Relations (A: 21 pp 400-406; B: 23 p. 371; C: 11 pp 272-273)
- Promotion (A: 15 and 19 pp 300-314 and 375-381; C: 11 pp 265-272)

REVIEW

Advertising (A: 16 and 17 pp 315-355; B: 23 pp 348-371; C: 11 pp 273-289)

"Multinational companies operating in a highly competitive environment depend more and more on their effectiveness in marketing and, in particular, on advertising to maintain their rate of growth. The decision facing international hotel firms, like all multinationals, is whether to standardize their message across different countries or to customize them in each location." S.J.Messenger and S.M.Lin, (IJCHM, v3n3, pp 28-32, 1991.)

The American Marketing Association refer to advertising as any paid form of non-personal presentation and promotion of ideas, goods or services by an identifiable sponsor.

The aim of advertising therefore, is to influence a person's knowledge, attitude and behaviour either in the short term or the long term.

Advertising is a deliberate and pre-determined form of communication. The firm spends money to communicate with the marketplace in order to meet specific objectives. The objectives determine the type of communication needed and the means of reaching customer groups. There are three different styles of advertisement which can be used to influence customers:

- *Informative advertising*. Mass-media communication with the aim of influencing the audience's cognitions about a product. Its purpose is educational, and its success can be measured by the ability of the audience to recall pieces of information and explain the content of the advertisement.

- *Persuasive advertising*. Mass-media communication with the aim of inducing purchasing behaviour.

- *Confirmative advertising*. Mass-media communication with the aim of reducing post-purchase dissonance. This or a feeling of uncertainty occurs when the anxiety experienced by the customer is greater than expected. It is typically associated with a moderate to high cost, infrequent purchase where the risks of making an inappropriate choice are higher than for more familiar, routine purchases.

Most advertisements contain elements of all three forms - informative, persuasive and confirmative.

Advertising is an element of the marketing mix and its objectives are derived in part from a mix of configuration needs and decisions. Further, it requires careful formulation so as to specify details of both the target audience and the desired effect.

Due to the high costs and difficulties of undertaking research into the sales effectiveness of advertising, marketers tend to set their objectives in relatively straightforward communication terms. These are exposure, awareness, and comprehension.

- *Exposure* to advertising is the least demanding of advertising objectives. The exposure effectiveness of an advertisement is measured by its reach, which is the total number of the target market audience exposed to the advertisement, and by its frequency, which is the average number of times a member of the target audience is exposed to the advertisement.

- *Awareness* is measured by the target customer's ability to recall advertising content.

- *Comprehension* is measured by the customer's ability to interpret the content of an advertisement in a meaningful way.

A secondary consideration in setting advertising objectives is the strategic situation of the product. This can be assessed in relation to: (a) the nature of the product; (b) the product life cycle (PLC) stage; and (c) the positioning of the product and its competitors.

(a) The nature of the product

Due to the characteristic features of intangibility, perishability, heterogeneity and inseparability, services face particular advertising problems. To overcome them, the following guidelines are helpful:

- Use clear, unambiguous messages.
- Emphasize benefits, not technical details of the service.
- Only promise what can be delivered.
- Advertise to employees too.
- Obtain and maintain customer co-operation during service delivery.
- Build on word-of-mouth recommendations.
- Provide tangible clues which give the intangible product a concrete dimension.
- Try to ensure the continuity of the advertising message.
- Seek to minimize sources of purchase dissonance.

(b) The PLC stage

The approach to advertising is likely to differ according to the stage of the product life cycle. In the introductory stage advertising should seek to encourage trial, raise awareness and ensure key benefits are clearly understood. During growth, priority should be given to supporting repeat purchasing, penetration of new segments, developing market share and widening distribution. At the maturity stage the priorities switch to maintaining market share, reinforcing brand image and establishing reasons for a price differential. At decline the focus is often on lengthening the life cycle through promotion to new segments.

(c) The positioning of the product and its competitors

Pricing and positioning are key determinants of the type of advertising and the approach used. 'Image' is an important intangible for high-priced luxury goods whereas the challenge for a 'me-too' product positioned alongside competitors is more likely to involve ensuring that key benefits are salient in the minds of customers.

If strong positioning is dependent on low pricing, it will be necessary to build a value-for-money, no-nonsense image.

The advertising budget defines the limit within which the media planner must operate and most organizations use the services of an advertising agency. The selection of the agency is a key decision, as the success of the campaign is largely determined by the creative component and the way in which the campaign is managed.

Public Relations

(A: 21 pp 400-406; B: 23 p. 371; C: 11 pp 272-273)
A number of marketing roles can be fulfilled by public relations (PR) for example:

"...improving awareness, projecting credibility, combating competition, evaluating new markets, creating direct sales leads, reinforcing the effectiveness of sales promotion and advertising, motivating the sales force, introducing new products, building brand loyalty, dealing with consumer issues and in many other ways."(1)

PR is a specialized activity that involves influencing audiences inside and outside the organization. Further, it has a corporate as well as a marketing role in promoting image and reputation.

PR can be undertaken both in-company and by consulting organizations on behalf of clients, and it is used in two ways by marketers. It has (a) a problem-solving role (the marketer, faced with a communications problem, finds a PR solution), and (b) a problem-avoidance role (prior to launching a new product, it is helpful to identify barriers to success and through PR, try to influence potential sources of opposition).

There are a wide range of PR techniques including: print media relations, radio and television relations, publications, special events, and community involvement. The most common form of PR in hospitality marketing is publicity - the provision of newsworthy stories normally taking the form of a news release and/or press pack to the print and broadcast media.

Buttle (A: 21 pp 401-402) cites five PR techniques which hospitality/tourism operators can utilise in order to gain publicity. These are:

(a) print media relations

The provision of materials for editorial use in the print media, including: news (or press) releases; press packs; letters to editors; meetings with editors; writing articles; provision of information for feature writers; establishing a press office; calling occasional press conferences and photocalls.

(b) radio and television relations
Using broadcast media to seek programme opportunities; radio interviews (by telephone or in the studio); television interviews; panel discussions.

(c) publications
Including leaflets; brochures; house journals; corporate publications; sponsored books; other print media (such as calendars, diaries, posters, wallcharts, stickers and leaflets).

(d) special events
Including seminars; exhibitions; openings/launches; celebrations; competitions; tastings; conferences; open days; familiarization tours; film shows; stunts and speeches.

(e) community involvement
Including events planned in conjunction with professional bodies; sports/social clubs; charitable organizations; schools and colleges.

Summarizing, PR is concerned with promoting the organization, its products, services and individuals by generating favourable publicity. The target publics are: the community, employees, government agencies, the financial community, distributors, customers, opinion leaders, and the media.

Promotion (A: 15 and 19 pp 300-314 and 375-381; C: 11 pp 265-272)

"Promotion marketers in the tourism industry must look beyond the immediate concerns of short-term sustainability and consider the strategic imperatives of making meaningful progress in the long run. The full value and potential of promotions cannot be realised if underlying concepts are forced to stop and start over a period of days, weeks or months. Building promotional equity depends on allowing big ideas to grow and improve over a period of years." P.Rita and L.Moutinho (IJCHM v4n3, 1992, pp. 3-8.)

The ultimate goal of all promotion is to obtain a level of demand which is favourable to the promoter - to increase, decrease, or maintain demand, and/or to influence the elasticity of demand by using channels of communication which allow access to a defined target audience. (A: 15 p. 300.)

The promotional mix is the set of communication tools which a marketing department can use in order to influence demand.

It includes:

- *Advertising.* Paid communication by an identified sponsor through a non-personal medium.

- *Selling.* Personal selling is paid face-to-face persuasive communication by an identified sponsor. Telephone selling is paid persuasive communication by an identified telephone caller.

- *Sales promotion.* Activity that triggers a temporary incentive effect and which is targeted to customers, channel members, or sales personnel.

- *Direct mail.* Postal communication by an identified sponsor.

- *Sponsorship.* The material or financial support of a specific activity, usually sports or the arts, with which the sponsor is not, in the normal course of business, associated.

- *Merchandising.* Activity that triggers or stimulates purchase interest or intent, other than personal selling, and which takes place at the point of sale.

- *Public relations.* The means by which the various significant publics of an organization are identified and communicated with, to the advantage of the organization, through personal and non-personal media.

- *Publicity.* Unpaid communication by an identified sponsor through non-personal media.

The methods used in promotional effort depend upon the objectives sought, the nature of the product, the type of distribution channel employed and the target audience. In the case of sales promotion, the marketer must establish the objectives, select the appropriate promotional tools, develop and implement the programme, and evaluate results.

Some forms of promotion are comparatively inexpensive or free (word-of-mouth recommendations, publicity and some forms of merchandising) and it is therefore sensible to fully exploit this potential. In setting the promotion budget, the organization must define how much it can afford to spend on its overall promotional effort, and how it can optimize return on expenditure in relation to the promotional mix.

CONCLUSION

"Motel advertising has been a source of comfort to the weary traveller seeking relief from the tedium of travel, a source of delight to the television viewer seeing the clever and witty advertisements of price-oriented motels, and a source of alarm to environmentalists viewing the imposing and grouped billboards on the arteries of the nation. To the owners and operators of the nation's motels, advertising is one of the marketing tools available for securing patronage." L.S.Lowe and A.Kruger (IJCHM, v3n1, 1991, pp 17-21.)

The key promotional challenge in hospitality and tourism advertising, public relations and sales promotion is to establish the most effective promotional mix so as to ensure optimal return on expenditure. Further, it is important to ensure that this component is properly integrated with the other components of the marketing mix, namely the product itself, pricing and distribution.

Reference:

1. R.Haywood. *All About Public Relations.* McGraw-Hill, London, 1984.

Review questions:

1. Identify the main styles of advertisement and the differences between them. Use hospitality and tourism examples where possible to illustrate differences of approach.

2. Evaluate the potential contribution of public relations to hospitality and tourism promotion. Cite examples to illustrate effective exploitation of PR opportunities.

3. Using hospitality/tourism examples, evaluate the various communication tools available to the marketer and explain how they can be used to influence demand.

EXTENSION

Read: 'Motel Advertising: Practices and Themes.' by L.S.Lowe and A.Kruger. *International Journal of Contemporary Hospitality Management*, Volume 3, Number 1, 1991, pp 17-21.

This article examines American motel advertising practices, methods of evaluation and key questions about their practices.

Key questions relate to: media selection for motel advertising; the dominant advertising themes; the relative importance of advertising agencies; advertising expenditure; the relative effectiveness of advertising and the extent to which motel location, ownership, size, number of chain-operated units and intensity of competition influence the advertising approach.

Note: If this article is not available in your library, select an alternative article to use in conjunction with the questions below.

Extension questions:

1. Evaluate the styles of advertising used by a selection of tour operators and test the comparative attractiveness of the sample adverts to students. How could the adverts be improved?

2. A hospitality/tourism organization is experiencing internal employee relations problems which are being exploited by competitors to the detriment of its public image. How would you use PR to counter the this situation?

3. An upscale (high spend) town centre restaurant is experiencing a decrease in its sales due to the impact of a campaign mounted by a new competitor located nearby. How would you define your promotional mix to combat the negative sales trend?

Practical exercises:

1. To what extent can companies in the fast food sector use informative advertising to combat public 'healthy eating' campaigns? Conduct a comparative review of the approaches used by at least *two* fast food chains.

2. Investigate the PR campaign used by a hospitality/tourism organization of your choice in association with a new product launch.

3. Prepare a promotional plan for a resort time-share organization which is facing tough competition from a nearby block of newly constructed self-catering apartments.

12
DIRECT MARKETING PERSONAL SELLING & MERCHANDISING

INTRODUCTION

"It is anticipated that the increase in competitive intensity that will be experienced in the hospitality industry of the 21st century will necessitate a greater emphasis on non-traditional forms of marketing."
S.Crawford-Welch (IJCHM, v3n3, 1991, pp 21-27.)

The effective use of techniques like direct marketing, personal selling and merchandising can help organizations to achieve improvements in competitive performance. The aim of this chapter is to examine the key principles and applications of these marketing mix elements.

In this chapter:
- Direct marketing (A: 19 pp 381-384)
- Personal selling (A: 18 pp 356-373; B: 24 pp 385-392; C: 12 pp 291-306)
- Merchandising (A: 20 pp 388-398)

REVIEW

Direct marketing (A: 19 pp 381-384)
Direct marketing is a form of sales promotion and distribution which can be defined as postal communication by an identified sponsor (1). Its many applications mean that it is a potentially powerful marketing communication tool.

The main advantages of direct marketing include:
- *Selectivity* - the messages can be tailored to suit target readerships from a single person to many thousands of recipients.
- *Personalization* - advanced computer-based databases can generate mail shots which address individuals in a personal way.
- *Limited competition* - postal deliveries do not produce the 'promotional noise' found in broadcast or press advertising.
- *Fewer mechanical restrictions* - the size, length and colour of postal communications are limited only by cost, what is practicable and what the potential customer is likely to read.

- *Convenient scheduling* - the production and delivery of direct marketing material offers complete flexibility.
- *Ease of response* - mail shot design can incorporate postage paid return postcards, envelopes, or coupons to make replies as easy as possible for the customer.
- *Ease of measuring effectiveness* - response rates are comparatively easy to monitor and measure for the purposes of determining cost and communication effectiveness.

There are a number of disadvantages associated with the use of direct marketing. These are:
- *Mailing list inaccuracies* - it is often difficult and time consuming to ensure that mailing addresses are accurately and routinely updated. Further, commercially available mailing lists do not always meet target market specifications.
- *'Junk-mail' image* - direct mail has become so popular that the impact and credibility of this form of marketing communication is more difficult to establish.
- *The need for copy-writing expertise* - to ensure that the direct mail message and content are appropriate to the communication medium, it may be necessary to employee the services of a direct marketing specialist.
- *Operating costs* - associated with postage, printing, paper, copy-writing and mailing list purchase and/or support should be calculated in relation to the expected rate of return. If response levels are low, it may be due to an operational error (such as a poorly-timed mail-out) or the possibility that a direct marketing approach is unsuited to the product and/or target market needs.
- *Postal regulations* - regarding size, weight and content may impede the communications effort and thereby invalidate the immediacy and impact of a direct marketing campaign.

Mailing lists for direct marketing purposes can be compiled internally or acquired from commercial vendors, sometimes known as list brokers. In this instance the user normally pays a broker for the right to use, but not buy a mailing list. Prices vary according to the list's exclusivity, cost of compilation and maintenance, demand, predicted response level and its level of accuracy and completeness as a free-standing information source. Access to up-to-date, exclusive lists with a proven, high rate of response is invariably more expensive.

The contents of a mail-shot will depend on the aims of the direct marketing campaign, but most mail-shots consist of four print items: (a) the mail-out envelope; (b) the offer letter; (c) the accompanying leaflet or brochure and (d) the return card or envelope. To improve the prospects of achieving a good response rate, several guidelines can be used to assess the overall impression of the direct mail materials at the design stage:

- Mail-out envelopes featuring an eye-catching logo or illustration stand a better chance of being opened;
- Personalize the offer letters (address and contents) where possible;
- Use conversational and credible copy to ensure that the message is easy to read and comprehend;
- Supporting materials such as leaflets and brochures should be succinct, concisely written using a simple design layout and attractive to look at and read;
- Key benefits and service guarantees should be built-in copy features of the leaflet or brochure;
- Supply pre-coded order forms together with freepost or reply-paid envelopes.

Like all components of the promotional mix, direct marketing requires careful planning by: (a) identifying opportunities; (b) establishing priorities; (c) defining target audiences and objectives; (d) budgeting; (e) deciding upon timings; (f) assigning responsibilities for implementation; and (g) selecting appropriate methods of monitoring and evaluating the direct marketing effort.

Personal selling (A: 18 pp 356-373; B: 24 pp 385-392; C: 12 pp 291-306)
Selling is a form of paid communication by an identified sponsor through a personal medium. More specifically it can be viewed as an interpersonal transaction whereby one or more parties seek to influence an exchange. Selling differs from advertising because it is a personal form of communication and from word-of-mouth promotion because it is a paid activity.

A selling function is performed by all employees who come into contact with customers. Specialist sales staff can be classified as internal or external employees or as agents. Employees sell only their employer's products, are subject to a contract of employment and are generally easier to direct and motivate. External agents, however, often sell competing products and act independently.

Regardless of title or classification, sales staff perform one or more of the following tasks:
- *Prospecting.* This involves locating and securing new sources of business.
- *Information distribution.* Sales staff initiate and/or participate in the dissemination of information about forthcoming events such as

advertising campaigns and new product and sales promotions internally and to prospective customers.
- *Information acquisition.* Sales representatives act as an intermediary, feeding back information about customer tastes or competitors' sales promotions and prices.
- *Client service.* Sales staff provide various forms of customer support which may include advisory work on financing a purchase or routine product maintenance and on-going support.
- *Selling.* The salesperson must be able to convert prospects into customers and maintain a long-term relationship, so that key marketing objectives relating to customer satisfaction and loyalty are achieved.
- *Administration.* Typical tasks include planning sales calls, writing-up call reports and submitting weekly/monthly summary reports to management.

The sales manager's job is to ensure that staff fulfil their assigned role as effectively and efficiently as possible. To achieve this, a number of organizational tasks must be completed and periodically reviewed. Key tasks include: (a) determining the sales force size; (b) determining the sales force structure; (c) selecting sales personnel; (d) designing the salesperson's job; (e) training salespersons; (f) devising remuneration systems; and (g) controlling, supervising, motivating and evaluating salespersons.

(a) Determining the sales force size
The size of the sales force will depend on the type of organization it represents and the range of products and services which require sales support. More specifically, the number of sales representatives is determined by the level of representation needed to ensure customers are effectively supported. A sales team representing a hotel chain can refer customer contacts to sales support or conference and banqueting staff at the individual unit level, but corporate customers represented by their key decision-makers should be regularly contacted by a member of the corporate sales team. To ensure that this happens, the sales team should be sufficiently large enough to service all key customer contacts and support efforts to locate new business.

(b) Determining the sales force structure
After deciding on the number of sales persons to employ, the next step is to decide how to deploy them. This can be done by geographical area, by product or product group or by customer type.

(c) Selecting sales personnel
Sales representatives constitute a valuable asset and it is important to recognise that successful

salespeople are likely to move between employers. It is therefore important to ensure that the financial incentives relating to an individual's sales performance are attractive and attainable. Additionally, career opportunities in marketing, sales and other organizational functions should be provided where possible, so as to retain key sales staff.

(d) Designing the salesperson's job
The key tasks include setting sales quotas, establishing sales territories, identifying key accounts and providing sales support.

(e) Training salespersons
To ensure that sales volume targets are met by the sales force, training and on-going personal development is required. This can be directed towards improving the performance of the sales person in the selling situation, or improving sales-support skills.

(f) Devising remuneration systems
Pay systems vary according to the company and the product or service sold but the most common forms of remuneration system are: salary only; commission only; and salary plus commission or other incentive. Ideally, the remuneration scheme should include a basic salary and performance-related pay or incentive element.

(g) Controlling, supervising, motivating and evaluating
Management systems play an important role in ensuring that objectives are achieved and problems are solved. Above all, it is essential to ensure that each member of the sales team is encouraged to optimize their selling potential for the organization by means of a fair and supportive framework which recognizes both effort and results.

Merchandising (A: 20 pp 388-398)

"Merchandising is any form of behaviour - triggering stimulus or pattern of stimuli, other than personal selling, which takes place at retail or other point of sale." (2).

Merchandising is best exemplified by its application to self-service retailing; its potential application to hospitality and tourism settings is not yet fully realized. In retailing terms this begins when a person enters a store and his/her movement around the display areas and shopping behaviour is partly conditioned by the way in which the retailer has planned the physical environment. A key objective is to trigger purchase intentions by displaying goods (or merchandise) as attractively as possible.

Advertising, public relations, direct mail and personal selling can be productive in bringing customers to hospitality outlets, thereafter merchandising assumes an important role in stimulating sales. Merchandising is essentially a non-personal promotion at the point of sale and its purpose is to stimulate short term interest in display items and ultimately to increase the average spend of the customer. This is achieved by stimulating or 'triggering' impulse purchases as the customer is exposed to well designed sensory stimuli.

Merchandising relies on three tactics to generate sales. These are: (a) accessibility; (b) sensory domination; and (c) appeal (or collectively 'ASDA'):

(a) Accessibility
Put simply, products which are accessible sell better than those which are not.

(b) Sensory domination
The main senses through which merchandising stimuli are received are sight, hearing, smell and touch. A product which attracts the attention of a prospective customer by dominating one or more of these senses is more likely to be bought.

(c) Appeal
Occurs when the potential customer feels attracted to the sensory stimuli and is motivated to buy. This often happens in an unplanned way if sensory stimuli trigger a need or feeling (such as hunger or thirst) and a reactive or 'impulse' purchase. There are a number of factors which influence the effectiveness of merchandising:

- *Low involvement purchasing.* When the purchase category is relatively unimportant (routine, low risk purchases) merchandising stimuli may be sufficient to stimulate variety seeking or new product trial.
- *Disposable income.* In general terms, higher levels of disposable income mean that people spend more in an unplanned way as they are less concerned about budgetary constraints.
- *Need fulfilment.* Merchandising can function by stimulating a need for social contact, status and authority, and thereby suggest a means of gratification.
- *Consumer values.* As societal values change, merchandising can inform customers as to how new values can be met through consumption.
- *Unplanned purchasing.* The shift towards self-service retailing recognises the importance of unplanned purchasing. A large proportion of this can be generated by exposure to merchandising stimuli.

Merchandising relies on the use of a range of media types. These can be classified as: (a) visual (such as displays, signs, posters, menus); (b) audio (using public address systems or promotional inserts in radio broadcasts); and (c) audio-visual (such as film, tape/slide and video presentations). The many possible combinations of stimuli require a carefully planned approach with measurable objectives and a rationale for the selection of merchandising techniques.

CONCLUSION

"Classical advertising has traditionally been the dominant player in the marketing mix. It is indeed a powerful tool. The 1990s, however, will see the final disappearance of the 'above and below the line' distinctions that have divided advertising from the other, perceived as less glamorous, activities like sales promotion, direct marketing and public relations." (3).

Direct marketing offers the benefits of selectivity, a personalized appeal and cost-effectiveness because it is comparatively easy to monitor. *Personal selling* provides an interpersonal influence on the exchange, and *Merchandising* aims to increase average expenditure through impulse purchasing. These three techniques can make an important contribution to attaining sales performance improvement.

References:

1. R.Wilson, C.Gilligan and D.Pearson. *Strategic Marketing Management: Planning, Implementation and Control.* Butterworth-Heinemann, Oxford, 1992.
2. F.Buttle, 'How Merchandising Works.' *International Journal of Advertising*, 3, 1984.
3. The Economist Intelligence Unit. *Marketing 2000: Critical Challenges for Corporate Survival.* EIU Management Guide, London, 1991.

Review questions:

1. Write a set of criteria to judge the value of a mailing list for a selection of hospitality /tourism services.

2. Devise outline specifications which could be used to evaluate the performance of the sales team in a hospitality/tourism organization of your choice.

3. Select a hospitality/tourism organization and critically evaluate its merchandising. Comment on the media it employs, and suggest others which you consider might be productive.

EXTENSION

Read: 'Marketing Hospitality Into the 21st Century.' by S.Crawford-Welch. *International Journal of Contemporary Hospitality Management*, Volume 3, Number 3, 1991, pp 21-27.

The article provides an overview of the importance of taking a different stance towards the pressing issues facing contemporary hospitality marketing. It addresses competitive conditions in the hospitality industry, and considers new directions for marketing.

Note: If this article is not available in your library, select an alternative article to use in conjunction with the questions below.

Extension questions:

1. What are the benefits and drawbacks to hospitality/tourism managers and organizations of using a direct marketing approach?

2. How should an organization measure the effectiveness and efficiency of its sales force, and the related sales management role?

3. How might some of the contemporary challenges for hospitality marketing identified by Crawford-Welch be addressed by the techniques reviewed in this chapter?

Practical exercises:

1. As sales manager for a tour operator you have been asked to draw-up a direct marketing plan for a new 'summer sun' holiday destination. Justify your proposals in a presentation to the senior management team.

2. Examine and evaluate the sales force structure of a tourism/hospitality organization known to you.

3. Prepare a merchandising plan for a tourism/hospitality organization, using a combination of visual, audio and audio-visual merchandising media.

13
INFORMATION SYSTEMS

INTRODUCTION

"Experience suggests that the marketing information area is more significant than we normally think. I would say that it is the single area where you can make the greatest and most significant difference to marketing strategies, programmes and customer satisfaction." (D: 6 p.174.)

Information offers this potential because it spans many areas from survey results, facts and figures to computerized databases. In essence, marketing information provides a means of understanding, interpreting and responding to the customer and the competitor. Its impact is felt throughout the organization and it can be used in a positive way to influence how people *think* about the market and, ultimately how they *respond* to it.

This chapter considers the role of marketing information and the need for a systematic approach to the collection, analysis and dissemination of data.

In this chapter:
- The role of marketing information (D: 6 pp 175-177)
- Marketing information: myths and reality (D: 6 pp 187-196)
- Marketing information, power and politics (D: 6 pp 197-207)
- Marketing information systems (D: 6 pp 178-187; B: 10 pp 179-194; C: 5 pp 99-138)
- Managing marketing intelligence (D: 6 pp 207-216)

REVIEW

The role of marketing information
(D: 6 pp 175-177)
Information is *the* vital ingredient in all marketing decisions - ranging from research and planning to strategy implementation. But there are several other reasons why the information function is central to the work of the marketing department. They relate to the intrinsic value and competitive gain that can be delivered by information systems.

(a) Marketing is an information function - as it spans the interface between the company and the customer. So, collecting, processing, analyzing and disseminating information about the marketplace is a routine activity.

(b) Information warrants responsibility - as business environments and information technologies are subject to dynamic change. Consequently there are more sources of marketing information and an ever-growing volume with rapidly improving access times. Management responsibility for marketing information and for planned information strategies should therefore be a high priority for the organization as a whole.

(c) Information is a marketing asset - because it affects the extent to which customer needs, attitudes and behaviour are understood. Further, it affects customer responsiveness, the ability to identify new market opportunities and the extent to which competitor threats can be anticipated.

(d) Information provides competitive advantage - as information systems affect the level and sophistication of customer service support. American Airlines and Thomson Travel among others, have successfully linked company information systems to on-line terminals so customer inquiries can be dealt with speedily. Information technologies can also be harnessed to provide forms of competitive differentiation (e.g. faster information services) information-based products (e.g. sophisticated hotel guest databases) improved marketing techniques and new marketing distribution channels via database marketing.

The importance of these issues should not be under-estimated and to ensure this, senior managers must take responsibility for the marketing information system and its development. In this respect, relentless technological advancement is helping to ensure that the information function is given priority attention. There is however, a need for caution - information systems are always imperfect and they do not in themselves make decisions. In reality formalized systems and widespread computerization can create both unrealistic expectations and inflexibility. Commenting on this, Paul Gamble puts the case for a balanced approach to the management of information and technology:

"The obstacle that the hospitality industry has encountered, in common with many others, is that the emphasis in the management of information technology has been on the technology itself rather than on the information.

The lip service that is paid to information as a resource of equal importance to personnel or finance is not recognized. Many companies produce budgets and business plans, some also produce manpower development plans but there are very few that produce IT plans. Even those that do are often more concerned with computing machinery than with information." (P.R.Gamble, IJCHM, v3n4, 1991, p.41.)

Marketing information: myths and reality
(D: 6 pp 187-196)

It is argued by Piercy among others, that a gap exists between an idealistic view of the role of marketing information and reality. Further, if misconceptions are allowed to persist, they may affect levels of confidence in the information function and commitment to improving the way in which the resource is managed and used throughout the organization. First then, it is helpful to examine the myths that surround marketing information.

(a) We need more marketing information. This wrongly assumes that by giving managers *more* information they will make better decisions. Piercy notes that 'information overload' can, if anything, impede decision-making (see D: 6 pp 189-190 for symptoms of information overload).

(b) We need marketing information more quickly. This is certainly possible given advancing technology, but is it desirable? The ability to monitor restaurant or bar sales using retailing technology like electronic point-of-sale scanning devices is now possible. Incoming 'real time' data *is* helpful but will it ever be necessary to produce hourly results? More to the point will managers then spend all their time computing results when in fact statistics produced on a sessional or daily basis provide adequate information support?

(c) If we try hard enough, we can know everything. A seductive idea, which invariably leads to the use of ever faster and more powerful computers. But in reality the most important information rarely exists when it is most needed. Further, accessing information at the top of the organizational decision-making pyramid becomes more difficult due to its confidentiality. So, attempts to correlate or compare data sets from the operational level which is readily available, with the strategic level, which is not, will almost certainly be frustrated.

(d) We know what marketing information we want. A response from managers which is often difficult to accommodate.

There are several reasons for this - first, even managers at the same organizational level use information in different ways. Second, decisions made at the strategic level in organizations are likely to involve complex variables and the predictability of information needs becomes much more difficult. Third, in reality information needs are often obscured by fuzzy, unclear and unquantified objectives, difficulties in identifying options and by uncertainty about external market forces. It may also be difficult to separate or isolate decisions from each other. These among other reasons, mean that organizations cannot predict precisely what information they need.

(e) We know why we want the information. The answer is simply to make better decisions. But for what purpose is the information needed? It could be for any of the following reasons: to *justify* decisions already made; to provide *reassurance;* to *signal* an intention for rational or political reasons; to build consensus about something; to *delay* or *prevent* a decision; to *reconcile* or *conciliate* diverse viewpoints; to establish *'ownership'* of a particular issue; or to gain *influence.* So, motives can and do influence information needs and in this sense access to information has many possible consequences.

(f) Well, we know what we don't need to know. This issue can skew the way in which information is collected and disseminated. The sources of information which are ignored, discarded or discredited in themselves illuminate aspects of organizational dogma, stereotyping and the key strategic assumptions that have been made.

(g) We measure what matters. In reality the evidence suggests that organizations tend to focus on what is easiest to measure.

(h) We know what we know. All too often managers have or adopt a narrow view of what is actually available in information terms. Is this culture of acceptance a healthy one? If not, progress can be made by seeking out sources of undisseminated information blockages to information flows.

(i) We know who decides what we know. This may appear ordered and reasonable, but formalized information systems may in fact, shield: (a) *constrained data sets* (are the criteria for selection widely known?); (b) *skewed data sets* (what impact will in-built biases and prejudices have?); (c) *static data sets* (is there anything new to be studied?); (d) *information games* (is information being used to manipulate and control situations and events?).

Marketing information, power and politics
(D: 6 pp 197-207)

There are principally three ways in which marketing information is used in organizations:

(a) As a controlling device - whereby 'ownership' of information is established and a power base is created by controlling access and interpretation of the data. This creates dependent relationships within organizations if one or more departments attain the status of 'official' keepers of key information. In turn, this can generate unproductive competition for control of critical information sources.

(b) As a political device - by filtering and manipulating marketing information so as to exert influence. It points to the existence of a 'hidden agenda' that has to be addressed before marketing plans and strategies will be accepted.

(c) As a rational resource - such that the role of marketing information is to provide objective research evidence, facts and figures that inform and support decision-making.

Marketing information systems
(D: 6 pp 178-187; B: 10 pp 179-194; C: 5 pp 99-138)

As noted earlier, computer-based systems should facilitate rapid access and transfer of information to users and decision-makers and a rational use of outputs from the marketing information system (MkIS) should provide an integrated view of a diverse range of information sources. Outlining the functions of the MkIS (D: 6 p 179) Piercy notes the following capabilities: storage and integration of information on marketing issues from many sources; regular dissemination to users; support for marketing decision-making in planning and control matters; sufficient scope to encompass (a) marketing productivity analysis, (b) marketing intelligence, (c) marketing research and modelling.

(a) marketing productivity analysis

A key test of marketing effectiveness is the relationship between inputs and outputs. For example, it is often difficult to equate advertising expenditure with sales yet this is an important statistic which, if known, can be used to justify expenditure. A computerized MkIS offers the capability to support creative and where appropriate, ad hoc interrogation of sales results, marketing cost ratios and elements of marketing cost accounting.

(b) marketing intelligence

A wealth of 'soft' or qualitative information exists which, if properly managed, will yield rich insights on market trends and provide background and context for statistical data.

Information sources include: personal experiences; sales staff reports; distributor feedback; trade and press articles and reports; government statistics; technical literature; meetings and industry gossip. Piercy notes that this type of information is often 'inaccurate, incomplete, sketchy, random, haphazard and unscientific' but that it is precisely the sort of information that managers use to make sense of the world in which they operate. There are two key implications of this, first that scope probably exists in most organizations for managing intelligence flows more *systematically* and second, a better understanding of how such intelligence is used will provide insights on how managers make *assumptions* about likely events.

(c) marketing research and modelling

The starting point for marketing research (MR) is *secondary research,* the logic being that if the information sought is already available, it is sensible to obtain and use it. If it isn't available, *primary research* to collect new data may be needed. Research design is influenced by the precise data needs, the most suitable way of obtaining the data and the size of the budget available. As discussed in Part 2, there are numerous ways of collecting data including: surveys, observations studies and various forms of product/market testing. The application of management science techniques to marketing information will support data modelling. Typical examples include simulation and forecast models, resource allocation models and expert system models.

Managing marketing intelligence
(D: 6 pp 207-216)

Marketing information has a direct impact on the formulation of plans and strategies. More specifically, it should reflect events in the external marketplace and the wider business environment. As noted in Chapter 7, *environmental scanning* is a technique which can be used to assess the impact of changes in the business environment on a company and its market(s). Further, it can provide a number of distinctive focal points for the purposes of analysis and evaluation. They include:

- *A focus on the competition* - to detect and assess direct competition for existing products and services ('me-too' competitors) and indirect competition (different products/services but with broadly the same customer appeal, thereby competing for the 'spend').
- *A focus on the legal environment* - to analyze the impact of new regulations on markets, exports, imports and other aspects of business.

- *A focus on the customer base* - to analyze trends relating to industry sectors, new product/service reactions, demographics, buyer behaviour and segment characteristics.
- *A focus on the new technology* - to identify potential impacts and applications in relation to customers, competitors, marketing channels, distribution, communications and techniques.

CONCLUSION

Piercy summarizes the role of information in marketing and more generally, in sustaining organizational activity:
"It certainly is true that collecting new information about customers, markets, competitors, and so on, can challenge our ideas and give us new insights into what matters most to customers. But this is only the tip of the iceberg. The big issues are more about: who decides what information we collect (and what we don't); what influences what information we believe and take notice of (and what we dispute and discard); what determines how 'objective' information is reported and used (and what is kept hidden and denied to decision-makers)?"
(D: 6 p.175.)

If organizations are to address 'the big issues' and meet their marketing information needs, a systematic approach to the collection, analysis and dissemination of data is needed.

Review questions:

1. Make a list of the information needs of a single unit hospitality/tourism owner-operated business. Use a series of diagrams and explanatory notes to show how routine and infrequent information needs and priorities can be met.

2. Explain the differences between marketing research and marketing intelligence data. To what extent can these activities be integrated?

3. Figure 6. 1 (D: 6 p. 179) depicts the marketing information system. To what extent can and should this information be shared throughout the organization as a whole?

EXTENSION

Read: 'CEO Perspectives on Scanning the Global Business Environment' by M.D.Olsen, B.Murthy and R.Teare. *International Journal of Contemporary Hospitality Management,* Volume 6, Number 4, 1994, pp 3-9.

This article reports on a survey of chief executives of multinational hotel chains. The purpose of the survey was to assess the environmental scanning practices in those hotel firms and learn how their executives view the uncertainty of the global business environment.

Note: if this article is not available in your library, select an alternative article to use in conjunction with the questions below.

Extension questions:

Assume that you are advising a multinational hospitality/tourism organization:

1. How should the activities of environmental scanning, marketing planning and marketing strategy be organized to take advantage of uncertainty in the business environment?

2. To what extent will 'green' issues and concern to preserve the natural environment impede marketing in the coming decade? How should the organization respond?

3. How should trends in the general, task and functional environments be monitored so as to assess the likely implications for marketing?

Practical exercises:

The following exercises should ideally be undertaken in small groups:

1. Select a national hospitality/tourism firm and conduct an assessment of the marketing environment in which it operates. Use the framework in Figure 6.6 (D: 6 pp 209-211) to structure your interpretation. Instructions for using the framework follow on pp 212-214.

2. Using Diagnostic 4 as a guide, (D: 6 pp 227-231) identify the marketing information needs of the firm by brainstorming information sources, gaps, barriers and problems.

3. Devise a marketing information system for the firm. This should include diagrams and explanatory notes together with details of information gathering priorities and timings (daily, weekly, monthly, periodically).

14
MARKET-LED STRATEGY

INTRODUCTION

"Strategic marketing planning is a 'hot' issue in many organizations today...there is widespread agreement that the big problem with marketing is not learning how to use sophisticated analytical management tools, computerized planning techniques, or even writing great innovative marketing plans - it is quite simply producing marketing plans and strategies that happen."
(D: 9 p. 322.)

Marketing strategy is concerned with the deployment of resources and the co-ordination of interactions with internal and external markets for the purpose of achieving specific objectives. This chapter examines the issues involved in devising and implementing strategy and it concludes by identifying the factors which influence the extent to which organizations are able to focus on customer needs through market-led strategic change.

In this chapter:

- Devising marketing strategy: A systematic approach (D: 3 pp 69-105)
- Relationships between planning and strategy for hospitality/tourism marketing (A: 7 pp 159-180; F: 6 pp 83-96; F: 12 pp 194-212)
- Implementing marketing strategy (D: 9 pp 321-364)
- Tactics for securing market-led strategic change (D: 9 pp 340-341; D: 11 pp 394-397)

REVIEW

Devising marketing strategy: A systematic approach (D: 3 pp 69-105)
Piercy notes that much of the writing and consultancy in marketing is concerned with issues of marketing strategy where the main theme relates to the direction of a business in its various marketplaces. This is a broad definition and put simply, it is about: (a) doing best what matters most to the customer; (b) achieving long-term customer satisfaction and, (c) finding new and better ways of responding to customers so that they remain *the* focal point for the marketing effort.

If marketing is to be effective, it is essential to define the tasks and interrelationships between strategy, action programmes and information needs. Piercy describes them as follows:

- *Marketing programmes* are concerned with actions in the marketplace. The key issues are (a) product policies; (b) pricing policies; (c) marketing communications; (d) distribution and service policies.

- *Marketing information* is needed to provide intelligence about the marketplace. The key issues are (a) information flows for planning and control; (b) marketing research; (c) marketing information systems.

- *Marketing strategy* is concerned with overall direction in the marketplace. The key issues are (a) mission analysis; (b) market definition; (c) market segmentation; (d) competitive differentiation and positioning; (e) matching marketing assets with customer needs.

(a) Mission analysis
Piercy's starting point in a logical sequence, is to establish the basic purposes (mission), determine specific goals (objectives), determine what needs to be done to achieve them (marketing strategies) and what specific action is needed in the marketplace (marketing programmes). Mission analysis has two dimensions:

- *customer missions* - focusing on customer needs and segments;

- *key value missions* - focusing on what is important to the organization and how it should be run.

The combined mission analysis helps to define: (a) the market from a customer perspective; (b) the different types of customer that exist; (c) the competitive position; (d) development opportunities relating to the customer base and marketing capabilities.

(b) Market definition
A periodic review of the specific issues which define target markets, namely products, services and customer types will yield insights on how the product-customer fit is evolving. Piercy's product-customer matrix (see D: 3 pp 82-83) can be used to examine trends, product life cycle issues, strategic positioning and market strengths.

(c) Market segmentation

A review of market segments can provide a means of identifying gaps that may exist and indeed be widening, between intended and actual customer benefits delivered to customers. It is also helpful to establish if particular market niches are expanding and if so, whether they may become viable market segments in the future.

(d) Competitive differentiation and positioning

According to Michael Porter (1) there are just two sources of competitive advantage; low cost and differentiation. These translate into three generic strategies:

- *Cost/price leadership* - when the source of competitive advantage is low cost and the competitive scope is broad.

- *Differentiation* - when the source of competitive advantage is differentiation and the competitive scope is broad.

- *Focus* - when the source of competitive advantage is either low cost or differentiation and the competitive scope is narrow.

The means of attaining competitive differentiation relate to the (a) product/service offering itself; (b) the value-added components (such as after-sales service) and (c) marketing intangibles like reputation, brand image and identity, word-of-mouth recommendations and perceptions of quality and value. Regardless of whether the scope of competition is broad or narrow, efforts to ensure that customers *perceive* a difference between the product offering and its rivals should be a standing priority. Piercy's 'competitive mapping' approach (D: 3 pp 95-97) illustrates how this can be achieved.

(e) Matching marketing assets to customer needs

The match between products, services, delivery capability and customer requirements is an endless quest because 'perfect fit' between the two rarely if ever, exists. The most logical way of tackling this problem is to drive the business by customer satisfaction management so that organizational structures become more closely aligned with market demand. There are two approaches which can be used to assist this endeavour:

- *asset-based marketing* - which emphasizes the need to find ways of exploiting existing assets more effectively in line with customer satisfaction expectations;
- careful use of *marketing assets* which, because they are usually intangible and difficult to monitor, warrant particular attention.

Relationships between planning and strategy for hospitality/tourism marketing

(A: 7 pp 159-180; F: 6 pp 83-96; F: 12 pp 194-212) Sirkis and Race (2) outline some of the inter-linking principles for planning and strategy. If strategy is to succeed, it requires realistic objectives founded in plans for the business as a whole or its composite parts. The latter are sometimes referred to as strategic business units or SBUs. Buttle illustrates the range of product-market relationships for an independent city-centre hotel. The hotel is itself an SBU and Figure 7.1 (A: 7 p. 162) identifies some of the options for its development.

It is usually helpful to examine the feasibility of options against key criteria such as relative market attractiveness. Several existing frameworks (or matrices) can be used for this purpose:

The Boston Consulting Group (or BCG) matrix
The BCG matrix assesses options against market growth and relative market share criteria. Market growth determines the ease and cost with which improvements in market share can be made; relative market share is a measure of cash-generating potential. The two criteria form the axes of a graph (see A: p. 165, Figure 7.3) with four quadrants which categorize the options. *Stars* require investment to achieve potentially good market share; *Cash cows* offer the prospects of good income for limited expenditure; *Dogs* indicate an untenable market position and *Question marks* if handled carefully may gain in strength (becoming a star) if not, market share may decline (becoming a dog).

The directional policy matrix (DPM)
The DPM uses the company's competitive capabilities and the business sector's prospects as axes. Competitive capabilities are judged as strong, average or weak relative to the company's market share, operational capability and product development policy. Each of the nine cells corresponds to a strategic option (see A: p. 166. Figure 7.4). Further examples and applications can be found in F: 6 pp 90-96.

After assessing the options, marketing strategy objectives can be formulated with reference to marketing mix policies such as product/service quality and pricing (see for example, A: p. 169, Figure 7.5). If the selected option(s) involve new market entry or development, it is necessary to assess the alternatives for implementing strategy. They include: (a) acquiring an existing hospitality/tourism business; (b) new build/purchase; (c) setting-up a management contract; (d) acquiring a joint venture; (e) establishing a joint venture with one or more partners.

(See F: 12 pp 194-212 for a discussion of these issues and marketing strategies used by hotel companies.)

Implementing marketing strategy
(D: 9 pp 321-364)

Market-led strategy and its implementation is the essence of effective marketing. Piercy argues that organizations constantly underestimate the degree and type of change that has to happen if marketing plans and strategies are to succeed. Further, he contends that a division is created by attempts to organize, staff, operate and organizationally separate these activities from the line management of the business. To test the resolve for implementing strategy he offers a model which mirrors organizational reality (D: p 335, Figure 9.5). This he likens to trying to fit a parcel (*the strategy*) through a hole in the wall (*the culture*) where issues like acceptance and resourcing may be constrained by procedures, controls and organizational culture. Marketing strategies and the actions needed to get them accepted, resourced and implemented are summarized below.

(a) Low risk strategies
These embody comparatively low priority issues and because of this, a patient approach is appropriate. They may succeed if they are presented at the right moment or if they are crafted so as to mirror the prevailing corporate mood. It may be appropriate to wait for 'part of the wall to crumble' which can happen if dominant individuals leave the organization or a rift occurs between a particular group of senior managers.

(b) Soft sell strategies
The tactics here may include submitting the strategy in incremental steps or re-submitting a rejected strategy by presenting the arguments, facts and figures in a different way. In both cases a bold (and possibly expensive) marketing strategy can seem more moderate and acceptable, especially if market-led change is at odds with the prevailing ethos and direction.

(c) Hard sell strategy
This approach requires a gathering of momentum through presentations, widespread involvement and ownership which will 'force it through the wall'.

(d) Gambles
If a proposal is known to be too expensive it may be possible to 'slide through' the more acceptable elements in the hope that once accepted, it will taken less effort to widen the hole in the wall than to amend or re-submit the proposal.

A variation on this is to present a big proposal and then unpack it to reveal a more modest one. Piercy suggests that this is probably the oldest managerial trick in the book but nonetheless an effective way of manipulating the culture while at the same time being seen to stick to the rules.

(e) Political strategies
This involves making the proposal more politically acceptable without changing either the strategy or the culture. One way of doing this is to ensure that the strategy is phrased using the latest, most acceptable corporate terminology (the 'flavour of the month'). A similar tactic is to involve or gain the support of members of the dominant coalition in the organization.

(f) Conflict strategies
An approach for confident managers and their teams or indeed for managers who feel that they have nothing to lose. It involves continually re-submitting the strategy until the argument (or battle) is won. It is probable that this confrontational approach will cause some re-shaping of both the strategy and the organizational barriers.

Tactics for securing market-led strategic change
(D: 9 pp 340-341; D: 11 pp 394-397)

In approaching one or more of the scenarios above there are certain ground rules which, if adhered to, will increase the chances of success. The key issues revolve around the following questions:

- *Basic objectives:* What is needed to make the strategy work? What resources are needed? Who controls them?
- *Problems:* What are the most critical elements? Who controls them? Who will co-operate? Who will resist?
- *Games:* What counter-implementation games are people likely to play?
- *Delays:* How much time should be built-in to account for delays? How much time will be needed for negotiations?
- *Support:* Which senior managers will provide support or help? Who could act as a political 'fixer'? Will one or more coalitions help? Will it be necessary to establish a 'contract for change' with key influencers?

CONCLUSION

The rationale for market-led change and for deploying the tactics needed to erode resistance to strategic change, is simply to re-focus on customers. Summarizing, Piercy re-states the nature of the challenge and affirms the need to 'champion' changes that will improve the effectiveness of the marketing system:

"Being market-led means putting the customer at the top of the management agenda, and using that as the focus for how we manage the organization and achieve our corporate objectives. It is about interpreting customer demands and needs to the key players inside the organization and changing their priorities. It is about the integration of all company activities and investments around what matters most to our survival - the customer...We have the tools to achieve this - marketing strategies, marketing programmes and marketing intelligence. We all too often do not use them very effectively, but they are there." (D: 11 pp 395-396.)

Market-led change offers the advantage of a consistent focal point (the customer) and the opportunity to ensure that change in marketing and throughout the organization is customer-led. This is arguably the best way of continually re-aligning products, services and organizational effort.

References:

1. M.E.Porter. *Competitive Advantage: Creating and Sustaining Superior Performance.* Free Press, New York, 1985.
2. R.L.Sirkis and S.M.Race. 'Principles of Strategic Planning for the Foodservice Firm', *Cornell Hotel and Restaurant Administration Quarterly,* 22 (1), May, 1981, pp 35-41.

Review questions:

1. Explain the links between marketing programmes, information and strategy. What action is needed to reinforce the 'fit' between marketing activity and the process of formulating and implementing marketing strategy?

2. Discuss the role of marketing planning in assessing strategic options. How can firms ensure that the planning process identifies the *right* marketing strategy at the *right* time?

3. Identify the likely reasons for resisting market-led change in hospitality/tourism organizations. How might they be overcome?

EXTENSION

Read: The 'Lion Machines Ltd.' case study in Chapter 9 of *Market-Led Strategic Change* (D: 9 345-356)

The case study provides a step-by-step practical approach to developing a market-led implementation strategy for marketing. It explains and illustrates the use of screening strategies for implementation problems; the value of using a priority/acceptability matrix; how to isolate and evaluate implementation strategies and the use of force-field and key player analysis.

Extension questions:

1. Devise your own set of actions and tactics (implementation strategy) for the 'Lion Roars in Water' strategy. Justify your proposals by stating your interpretation of the case study.

2. Write a report to Jim Patterson and George Watson with the aim of reconciling differences of approach (their proposals and yours) and advising them of the possible problems and sources of resistance to the implementation strategy. (You may wish to refer to D: 10 pp 383-385.)

3. Debate the advantages and limitations of Piercy's market-led approach. Is it equally applicable to hospitality/tourism firms? If not, state what modifications might be needed.

Practical exercises:

The chief executive of your university/college wishes to implement a new strategy: 'Quality, value and service' throughout the organization. He/she has asked your team to write a specification for the strategy and to devise a detailed implementation plan for student services, food, bar and retail outlets.

The following exercise should ideally be undertaken in small groups:

1. Using Piercy's implementation planning worksheets 1-4 (D: 9 pp 357-364) and guided by your strategy specification, devise an implementation plan.

2. Undertake an internal marketing evaluation to assess the implications for internal marketing strategy. Use Piercy's implementation planning worksheets 5-8 (D: 10 pp 386-393) to facilitate this.

3. Prepare and deliver a presentation to the chief executive and the university/college board which outlines your strategy proposal and details your implementation plan for student services, food, bar and retail outlets.

15
INTERNATIONAL MARKETING

INTRODUCTION

The hospitality and tourism industries have a substantial international dimension which requires constant attention by UK operators so as to attract business and holiday tourism in the face of tough competition from other countries. British tourism as an 'export' has been remarkably successful and has made a substantial contribution to the Gross National Product during the past three decades. In the 1990s the growth of the European Union, the dramatic changes in Eastern Europe and the economic ascendancy of the Pacific rim countries will continue to challenge governments and commerce alike by the need to respond with effective marketing action. This chapter aims to examine the issues which underpin successful international marketing effort.

In this chapter:
- Export marketing and overseas trade
  (B: 14 pp 229-253; F: 10 pp 164-165)
- Identifying export opportunities
  (C: 14 pp 324-329; B: 15 pp 257-263)
- Export or international marketing?
  (B: 15 pp 255-257; C: 14 pp 322-325; 339-341;
  F: 12 pp 198-199)
- Entering international markets
  (C: 14 pp 332-337; B: 15 pp 257-260)
- The marketing mix applied to international
  markets (C: 14 pp 332-337; B: 15 pp 259-260;
  F: 11 pp 175-193)
- Marketing in the European Union (B: 16 pp
  265-278; C: 14 pp 342-345; F: 12 pp 200-212)

REVIEW

Export marketing and overseas trade
(B: 14 pp 229-253; F: 10 pp 164-165)
The international marketplace provides one of the most challenging environments for the hospitality and tourism marketer. In 1990, the World Tourism Organization (WTO) estimated that world trade in tourism was probably in excess of £80 billion and still growing steadily despite economic recession in the main tourist generating countries. In general terms, despite Britain's own economic plight it is still one of the world's principal trading nations.

Four factors have determined the extent of trade: political stability, urbanization, relatively stable exchange rates and industrialization.

Export marketing is not the same as international marketing but the two are often confused and it is important to make the distinction between them. *Export marketing* refers to the marketing of products, produced in one or more countries, *in* other countries. *International marketing* on the other hand, gives weight to the development of business in a number of countries or regions, with a framework capable of incorporating the establishment of local manufacturing, distribution and marketing systems.

The greater proportion of overseas trade in the UK is limited to exports and only larger companies set up offices or operations abroad.

Identifying export opportunities
(C: 14 pp 324-329; B: 15 pp 257-263)
Hospitality and tourism companies have mainly adopted a reactive approach to overseas business. If the main sources of overseas visitors are generated from particular regions such as the Middle East or United States then the company may decide to adapt its product accordingly. This approach has created difficulties when events like the Gulf War, or the Libyan Bombing campaign resulted in reduced demand from tourist generating countries. Companies without a formal overseas export marketing strategy were unable to switch their attention to other countries quickly enough or even reinforce demand from existing client countries.

The value of a proactive, dynamic approach to export marketing even for individual customers, can be illustrated by hotels like the Chewton Glen in Hampshire. As a country house hotel it has been able to sustain high levels of room occupancy due in part, to its established sales network in the United States. The number of potential markets is large - more than 240 are listed in the United States Statistical Yearbook for example. Even countries with subsistence economies generate demand for food, drink and accommodation from trade and government delegations and conferences international air crews and other sources in their own countries and abroad.

A key factor to consider is market accessibility and the extent of tariff and non-tariff barriers to trade. A *tariff* is a tax on products or services crossing international frontiers and it can constitute a serious obstacle to trade.

The General Agreement on Tariffs and Trade (GATT) is an attempt to reduce the need for tariffs and assist world trade. Most countries are signatories but the issues involved are complex and discussions on the reform of the agreement are on-going. *Non-tariff* barriers include other forms of government action to restrict trade. These may include *quotas* for instance, restricting the amount of money that tourists can take out of a country, or an embargo on government conferences abroad.

There are a number of UK-based organizations (such as the British Tourist Authority and the British Overseas Trade Board) that provide assistance in the identification of export opportunities. Additionally, it is helpful to investigate some of the broader issues that affect export prospects. Further research should be considered in relation to the following headings:

- *Economic* - GNP/GDP, population figures, wage levels, distribution networks, inflation, resources.

- *Market* - size, stage in product life cycle, market penetration level or average consumption level.

- *Cultural* - material culture, social structure, family relationships, language, religion.

- *Political* - incentives for joint ventures, tariffs, stability.

- *Legal* - civil and criminal liability is the jurisdiction of each nation state; is national legislation generally supportive of overseas exporters and investors?

Export or international marketing? (B: 15 pp 255-257; C: 14 pp 322-325; 339-341; F: 12 pp 198-199)
A decision to move overseas, either to win business or obtain supplies is sometimes described in terms of the 'evolution' of a firm's operations. The Wells International Product Life Cycle (B: 15 p. 256) portrays the stages of overseas trade development in the following way:

Phase one	The firm innovates in the home market.
Phase two	The strength of the offering attracts overseas interest.
Phase three	Passive exporting takes place.
Phase four	Overseas demand prompts the firm to export actively.
Phase five	The creation of a strong foreign market leads to local production.

According to this explanation, sales remain fairly constant as each successive phase is reached. Alternatively, Lancaster and Wesenlund (1) cite evidence to suggest that sales figures increase as each phase is completed and the export market becomes more firmly established.

Entering international markets
(C: 14 pp 332-337; B: 15 pp 257-260)
After deciding to target a particular country, the company has to establish the best mode of entry and an appropriate marketing mix to support market entry. Kotler (2) identifies five broad choices of market entry:

- *Indirect export*. Involves less investment and no overseas organization to support and control. This is usually a passive arrangement reacting to overseas orders without a dedicated export department.

- *Direct export*. A more proactive approach, seeking orders overseas perhaps through an overseas sales office or agent.

- *Licensing*. The licensor enters an agreement with a licensee in a foreign market offering the right to use a trademark or logo for a fee or royalty. The licensor gains entry to an overseas market, often providing marketing support to the licensee. Variations on this legal arrangement include, management contracts or franchising. Hospitality and tourism organizations use all of these methods for overseas expansion.

- *Joint ventures*. Foreign investors join with local investors to create a new company. Some countries insist that foreign investors form a joint venture with the local investor owning as much as fifty-one per cent of the equity.

- *Direct investment*. As a company gains experience in an overseas market it may decide to invest directly in property, manpower and production facilities. This constitutes a greater risk but provides the company with greater flexibility in the longer term.

The marketing mix applied to international markets (C: 14 pp 332-337; B: 15 pp 259-260; F: 11 pp 175-193)
The country and method of market entry will influence the way in which the marketing mix is formulated. Some hospitality and tourism products can be transferred directly to other countries with only minor modification, as their authenticity is the reason for their appeal.

This is perhaps best illustrated by the success of standardized American fast food concepts in culturally diverse markets. There are however, a number of modification issues to consider relating to product, promotion and pricing decisions.

(a) Product modification
Keegan (3) identifies five possible options for market entry, each encompassing the marketing mix elements of product and promotion:

- *Straight extension* - this is the introduction of the product in the same form and with the same communications as used in the home market.

- *Communication adaptation* - here the promotional theme is modified but the product remains the same.

- *Product adaptation* - the product is modified but the promotional theme is maintained.

- *Dual adaptation* - the product and communications approach are both modified to meet specific market needs and constraints.

- *Product invention* - involves innovating or inventing new product variations for foreign markets. The risk may not be so great with service products if the core product can be authentically customized. Hilton International have successfully done this with their Japanese service brand *'Wa No Kutsurogi Service'* meaning 'comfort and service, the Japanese way'. It consists of distinctive service features and special amenities appealing to both Japanese business and leisure travellers (4).

(b) Promotion
Language differences alone can preclude direct transfer of the communication mix to an overseas market. Further, straight translation may not be appropriate as the cultural, political and religious climate, customs, traditions and values require careful evaluation. Additions to the communication mix such as representation at exhibitions and trade fairs may also be appropriate.

(c) Pricing
Pricing policy must reflect costs and expected returns, but additional factors may need to be considered:

- *The price* - should be set according to the needs and requirements of the overseas market, and this may need to be reflected in product and promotional adjustments.

- *The terms of payment* - by overseas customers will need to be considered as should the means of payment (such as bank transfers, money orders or drafts). These issues also affect pricing policy decisions.

- *The currency and exchange rates* - of the agreement(s) and the extent to which funds can be repatriated (that is returned to the home country) are important issues to be resolved prior to confirming the pricing schedule. Further, when a company operates in several countries it may wish to transfer funds between them. Additional revenue can be gained or lost by trading on currency exchange rates.

Marketing in the European Union (B: 16 pp 265-278; C: 14 pp 342-345; F: 12 pp 200-212)
The advent of the European Union (EU) provides a significant trading opportunity for the UK. At the present time, trade with the EU represents over sixty-five percent of overseas trade. The hospitality and tourism industries with their in-built internationalism are uniquely placed to take advantage of this large and culturally diverse free market area. Marketing in the EU is greatly assisted by:

- Lower costs arising from the elimination of frontier controls.

- Improved efficiency from standardized trading regulations.

- Greater potential for exploiting economies of scale relating to the expansion of trade in overseas markets.

- Easier transfer of resources, including finance and personnel.

CONCLUSION

International and export marketing is a sophisticated, complex and resource-consuming practice, but hospitality and tourism companies wishing to extend their trading base must devote the necessary time and attention to researching and then targeting overseas markets. With the deregulation of trade throughout Europe, foreign hotel companies like as Accor have increasing their presence in the UK marketplace and may continue to do so. Companies based in the UK, especially those with substantial assets in the home market like Forte plc, are seeking to take advantage of European deregulation. Static or slow growth in UK domestic markets coupled with fierce competition for business are also compelling reasons for international expansion.

It is unlikely however, that all companies will expand by direct investment in overseas markets, some may prefer to enter contractual arrangements by joint venture or licence in order to take advantage of local expertise and reduce the risks of costly market entry. But there is no doubt that international markets will dominate the thinking of multi-national hospitality and tourism firms. The scenarios are many and complex, but the following analysis provides a thought-provoking summary of the present and future opportunities for international marketing:

"China is changing quite rapidly, despite recent setbacks...Latin America has to change rapidly, and this will be facilitated by the USA because America's economy is declining. We are likely to see the forging of some very large and powerful trading relationships consisting of the USA and Latin America, Japan and China, and Europe...If these three large and powerful trading blocs do develop, they will dominate global business transactions." (6) Bernd Chorengel, President & Chief Executive, Hyatt International Corporation.

References:

1. G.A.Lancaster & I.Wesenlund, 'A Product Life Cycle for International Trade: An Empirical Investigation', *European Journal of Marketing*, 18 (6/7), 1984, pp 72-89.

2. P.Kotler. *Marketing Management, Analysis Planning, Implementation and Control*, 7th ed., Prentice Hall, NY, 1991.

3. W.J.Keegan, 'Multinational Product Planning: Strategic Alternatives', *Journal of Marketing*, January, (33), 1969, pp 58-62.

4. A.Bould, G.B.Breeze and R.Teare, 'Culture, Customization and Innovation: A Hilton International Service Brand for the Japanese Market' in Teare R., and Olsen M.D., (Eds) *International Hospitality Management: Corporate Strategy in Practice*, Pitman, London and John Wiley, New York, 1992 pp 221-227.

5. B.Chorengel and R.Teare, 'Developing a Responsive Global Network of Hyatt Hotels and Resorts' in Teare R., and Olsen M.D., (Eds) *International Hospitality Management: Corporate Strategy in Practice*, Pitman, London and John Wiley, New York, 1992 pp 339-345.

Review questions:

1. Identify the export opportunities for the hospitality/tourism industries in your region.

2. Discuss the options for market entry that a company may have when considering international expansion.

3. Evaluate the possible changes to a three star hotel operator's marketing mix prior to implementing a plan to operate a hotel in France.

EXTENSION

Read: Chapter 12 of *Strategic Hospitality Management (Changes in international hotel companies' strategies)* (F: 12 pp 194-212)

This chapter examines changes in the hotel marketplace during the past thirty years with respect to internationalization and indicates the competitive challenges confronting the industry during the nineties.

Extension questions:

1. Explain the development of multinational hotel companies with reference to Porter's model of competitive strategy.

2. Evaluate the role of American companies in the development of the international hotel business.

3. Investigate current market trends and explain how prevailing market forces may affect hotel companies operating in the international marketplace.

Practical exercises:

1. Select a country and gather as much information as possible in approximately two hours from published sources. Establish basic information such as population size and density (extent of urbanization), infrastructure, cultural dimensions and principal economic activities.

2. Using a hospitality/tourism organization of your choice, outline how your recommendations for entering the marketplace of the country identified in (1) above. You can assume that there are no restrictions on the mode of market entry. Include a discussion of the marketing issues that your plan entails.

3. Prepare an outline communications plan for the task defined in (2) above.